I Can Problem Solve

ICPS

PRESCHOOL

SECOND EDITION

D1257541

An Interpersonal Cognitive Problem-Solving Program

Myrna B. Shure

I Can Problem Solve® is a registered trademark of Myrna B. Shure.

Research Press   2612 North Mattis Avenue   Champaign, Illinois 61822   (800) 519-2707   www.researchpress.com

Illustrations by Herbert Wimble and Joseph Mingroni
Cover design and illustration by Doug Burnett
Composition by Wadley Graphix Corporation
Printed by Malloy Lithographing

ISBN 0-87822-457-2
Library of Congress Catalog No. 00-133939

This program is dedicated to George Spivack,
my friend and research collaborator of 25 years.

CONTENTS

PROBLEM-SOLVING SKILLS

LIST OF COMPLEMENTARY APPLICATIONS

ACKNOWLEDGMENTS

This program is a revision of a curriculum originally designed in 1971. The research phase of program development was funded by Hahnemann NIH institutional daughter grant #720–20–0150, awarded to Myrna B. Shure, and by NIMH grant #RO–1–MH20372, Washington, DC, to Myrna B. Shure and George Spivack, and was conducted in cooperation with Dr. Milton Goldberg, then Executive Director of the Early Childhood Programs, School District of Philadelphia.

Special thanks go to George Spivack, whose initial research with adolescents demonstrated a clear association between interpersonal cognitive problem-solving skills and behavior. His vision—that enhancing interpersonal thinking skills could reduce or prevent high-risk behaviors—inspired the creation of day-by-day lesson-games to reach those goals. George's help and guidance were instrumental in identifying age-appropriate skills and paved the way for the present program for the preschool years.

I am deeply grateful to those who were, at the time of our original program development, administrators of the Philadelphia Get Set Day-Care Program, whose support and help made our work possible: Dr. Jeffrey O. Jones, Director; Rosemary Mazzatenta, Assistant Director; Dr. Lafayette Powell, Chief of Psychological Services; and Vivian Ray, Chief Psychologist. Special recognition goes to the Get Set Day-Care teachers who conducted and improved the program: Richard Benowitz, Mary S. Cochran, Jean Fargo, E. Delores Flint, Loretta E. Howard, Alice Jones, Molly McLaughlin, Mary Seiss, Sally Silver, Pamela Wilson, and Sandra B. Williams.

Thanks also to research assistants Marsha Bloom, Rochelle Newman, and Stan Silver for their creative contributions during the entire research effort. In addition, gratitude is due secretaries Valerie Stokes and Doreen Waller for their tireless efforts and calm responses to never-ending deadlines.

A very special thank you to everyone at Research Press, particularly to Ann Wendel, President, Russell Pence, Vice President of Marketing, and Dennis Wiziecki, Advertising Manager, for their belief in and enthusiasm for ICPS programming in the schools; to Suzanne Wagner, for her design of the pages, which makes them pleasing to look at and easy to read; and to my editor, Karen Steiner, who in her own inimitable style of ICPS let me know that "There's more than one way" to express a thought. Karen's careful attention to the littlest details and her patience with my never-ending questions made me feel safe and secure.

But it was that disarming troupe of critics, age 4, whose responses (and nonresponses) provoked constant change in the program. It is an open question as to whether they or I learned more.

INTRODUCTION

Every day, some kind of interpersonal problem arises between children, a child and a teacher, or a child and other authority figures. Some children can cope with and solve these kinds of problems very well; others appear less able to think them through. Over 20 years of research has shown that, as early as age 4, children can learn that behavior has causes, that people have feelings, and that there is more than one way to solve a problem. They can also decide whether an idea is or is not a good one.

This volume, along with two companion volumes designed for kindergarten-primary and intermediate elementary grades, shows teachers how to help children learn to solve the problems they have with others.* The program outlined in this book was originally developed for 4-year-old children in a preschool setting; the early language and feeling-word concepts can also be followed by most 3-year-olds.

The approach employed, originally called Interpersonal Cognitive Problem Solving, has come to be called I Can Problem Solve (ICPS) by the many adults and children who have used it. Although children with serious emotional disturbances will likely require more individual attention and/or outside professional help, ICPS offers a practical approach to help most children learn to evaluate and deal with problems. Its underlying goal is to help children learn *how* to think, not *what* to think. It does not tell them what to do when conflict or other problem situations come up. Rather, it gives children ways to talk about their view of problems and think problems through. The main goal, focus, content, method, and benefits of ICPS are summarized on the following page.

As this summary suggests, the benefits of ICPS training are numerous. Research has shown that when children learn to use problem-solving thinking, their social adjustment improves, with significant reductions in nagging and demanding, emotional upset, and social withdrawal. Children become more able to wait, share, and take turns, as well as to get along with others. Regardless of temperament, children become better liked and more aware of—even genuinely concerned about—the feelings of others. In brief, children who have learned the ICPS concepts are more successful in getting what they want when they can have it and are better able to cope with frustration when they cannot. Finally, ICPS not only helps lessen problem

---

*The other volumes in the program, *I Can Problem Solve: An Interpersonal Cognitive Problem-Solving Program (Kindergarten and Primary Grades)* and *I Can Problem Solve: An Interpersonal Cognitive Problem-Solving Program (Intermediate Elementary Grades)*, are also available from Research Press. For information about immediate and long-term scientific research findings, as well as about measures of alternative solution skills and consequential thinking skills, contact Dr. Myrna Shure, Drexel University, 245 N. 15th St., MS–626, Philadelphia, PA 19102.

THE ICPS PROGRAM

GOAL　　To teach children thinking skills that can be used to help resolve or prevent "people" problems

FOCUS　　Teaches children *how* to think, not *what* to think
Guides children to think for themselves
Teaches children how to evaluate their own ideas
Encourages children to come up with many solutions to problems on their own

CONTENT　　**Pre-Problem-Solving Skills**
Learning a problem-solving vocabulary
Identifying one's own and others' feelings
Considering other people's points of view
Learning cause and effect

Problem-Solving Skills
Thinking of more than one solution
Considering consequences
Deciding which solution to choose

METHOD　　Teaches skills through the use of games, stories, puppets, and role-playing
Guides the use of skills in real-life situations
Integrates ideas into other cognitive skills
Includes parent participation

BENEFITS　　**For Children**
Fun for children—presents lessons in game form
Builds self-confidence
Builds listening skills
Encourages generation of alternative solutions
Provides skills to handle new problems
Facilitates social interaction among peers
Teaches skills applicable to other situations
Increases sensitivity to others, sharing, and caring
Increases independence
Increases ability to wait
Increases ability to cope with frustration
Decreases impulsivity
Decreases social withdrawal

For Teachers
Reinforces other curriculum goals
Creates a more positive classroom atmosphere
Decreases time spent handling conflicts
Enhances teachers' own problem-solving skills

behaviors, but 1- and 2-year follow-up studies suggest that it can actually prevent their occurrence.

Evidence that the program is having an impact becomes noticeable to the teacher as children begin to use the language of problem solving in the classroom. During the early weeks, most children will begin to adopt the initial verbal concept skills outside of formal training, although it is not until later in the program that children begin to solve interpersonal problems on their own.

Some inhibited children will begin to speak up after only 2 or 3 weeks of the program, and many start relating to others by the end of the first 2 months. Changes in impulsive behavior take somewhat longer to occur, but most children show signs of increased patience, reduced emotionality, and readiness to talk things over before the final lesson is conducted.

As they learn the ICPS skills and how to use them, impulsive youngsters become less aggressive, less emotional in the face of frustration, and less impatient. Inhibited youngsters become less withdrawn and better able to stand up for their rights. At program's end, some youngsters may still act aggressively or impulsively, but they will have begun to talk about what they do in a way that indicates overt behavior change will soon follow. Although it takes time for such major behavior changes to occur, teachers find that helping children learn to think for themselves is well worth the effort.

PROGRAM OVERVIEW

The ICPS program for preschoolers includes both formal lessons and specific suggestions for incorporating ICPS principles in classroom interactions and the curriculum. Ideas to help parents apply the principles are also presented.

ICPS Lesson Content

Each of the 59 ICPS lessons contains a stated purpose, list of suggested materials, and a teacher script. The teacher script, intended as a flexible guideline, explains the basic steps in conducting the lesson. Most lessons take about 20 minutes. With one lesson presented each day, all can be completed in approximately 4 months.

As the outline on the following page shows, the lessons are grouped into two major categories: pre-problem-solving skills and problem-solving skills. The ICPS words and other pre-problem-solving concepts set the stage for the problem-solving skills, which are associated with alternative solutions, consequences, and solution-consequence pairs.

The vocabulary taught in the pre-problem-solving phase of the program plays a critical role in later problem-solving thinking. In the lessons, as in the following paragraphs, these words are capitalized to suggest the emphasis they should be given. First, the words IS and NOT help children later think, "This IS a good idea; that is NOT." Subsequently, children learn the meanings of the words SAME and DIFFERENT. These words help children understand, for instance, that hitting and kicking are kind of the SAME

OUTLINE OF ICPS LESSONS

LESSONS	PURPOSE
	Pre-Problem-Solving Skills
1–10	To teach the following ICPS word concepts: IS, SOME-ALL, NOT, OR, AND, and SAME-DIFFERENT
11–18	To help children learn to identify their own and others' feelings of being HAPPY, SAD, and ANGRY
19–22	To encourage skills associated with listening and paying attention
23–28	To introduce the ICPS word concepts WHY-BECAUSE (to help children begin to become aware that behavior and feelings have causes) and MIGHT-MAYBE (to help children avoid quick and faulty assumptions about others)
29–31	To encourage recognition of individual differences and to teach children to find out about people's preferences by asking, "Do you like?"
32–33	To help children understand what is FAIR and NOT FAIR and to illustrate that fairness sometimes means having to wait
	Problem-Solving Skills
34–38	**Alternative solutions:** To help children recognize what a problem is and learn ways to generate many possible solutions
39–50	**Consequences:** To help children learn to think sequentially as a prerequisite to understanding cause-and-effect relationships (Lessons 39–45) and to encourage actual consequential thinking (Lessons 46–50)
51–59	**Solution-consequence pairs:** To give children practice in linking a solution with a possible consequence in a one-to-one fashion

because they both involve hurting someone. Children can also begin to think, "I can think of something DIFFERENT to do." Other lessons help children identify their own and others' feelings, understand that there is more than one way to find out how someone feels (by watching, listening, or asking), and comprehend that DIFFERENT people may feel DIFFERENT ways about the SAME thing.

These basic ICPS word concepts not only help children recognize and find out about others' feelings, they suggest ways these feelings may be influenced. Considering people's preferences is one of these ways. Young children often assume others like the SAME things they do (often leading to faulty conclusions and, therefore, unsuccessful solutions). Through the lessons, children come to appreciate that if one way to make someone feel HAPPY is not successful, it is possible to try a DIFFERENT way.

As a precursor to consequential thinking, a lesson on the words WHY and BECAUSE helps children appreciate the impact of what they do on themselves and others. This understanding will help them later on to think, for instance, "He hit me BECAUSE I took his toy." Inasmuch as the effects of one's actions on another are never a certainty, the words MIGHT and MAYBE are introduced. Building up to the final problem-solving skills, other lessons concern what people like and how people feel when deciding how to solve an interpersonal problem, whether an idea IS or is NOT a good one BECAUSE of what MIGHT happen next, and the notion that there are lots of DIFFERENT ways to solve the SAME problem.

Conducting ICPS Lessons

Teachers have found the following suggestions for conducting ICPS lessons helpful with preschool children:

1. Present the lessons to the children as "games" in which they have a chance to learn and practice new skills. You may wish to spend no more than 5 to 10 minutes a day on initial lessons, slowly increasing the length of sessions to about 20 minutes. This helps children adjust to the program and gradually increase their attention span.

2. Vary the wording of the teacher script to suit your group. Flexibility of content is encouraged as long as the concepts to be taught are not lost. It is not necessary to memorize the script. You may wish to place it on your lap, on the floor, or on a table and casually read from it. Once you get comfortable with the ICPS style of eliciting responses, you may be able to get along without the script at all.

3. If possible, divide the class into groups of 6 to 8 children, some boys, some girls. Because ICPS involves a good deal of child response, each group should have some quiet and some talkative children. A whole group of nonresponders would likely result in group silence. Two particularly disruptive children who are friends should be placed in separate groups. Specific techniques for handling "difficult" children are included in the lessons themselves, as well as in Appendix C in this volume.

4. Children can sit in chairs or on the floor, but a semicircle is preferable to a straight line. Quieter or more inhibited youngsters should sit in front or near a teacher aide.

5. A teacher aide can assist in a number of ways. He or she can participate in the lesson and help by keeping the more disruptive children nearby to maintain interest and by occasionally encouraging the more inhibited youngsters to whisper a response. If the group is larger than 6 to 8 children, the aide may need to stay with the other children in the class during the period of formal training. Alternatively, the aide can train a second group at the same time. Even if the aide does not participate in the formal lessons, he or she can apply the concepts during the day when real problems arise. A consistent approach by teacher and aide will help the children apply their learning.

6. The group does not need to be sitting quietly "at attention" before a lesson begins. If you begin the lesson with a fast, exciting pace, the children generally settle down and participate.

7. If the group becomes restless early in a session, try an earlier lesson or a game such as Simon Says. If the group remains restless after returning to the lesson, stop for the day. Do not feel you must finish the day's lesson if the group is not with you. On the other hand, if the children are already familiar with the concepts, you may wish to move through the lessons more quickly. Because each lesson is a necessary part of the sequence, do not skip them entirely. Adjust the pace according to the needs of your own group.

8. If your class is having problems in grasping a particular concept, this need not be a stumbling block. The program includes ample repetition of specific concepts, and most children will eventually learn them. For this reason, a child who misses a day or two of training need not be "caught up" individually.

9. In some lessons, expect a high level of verbal participation. The goal is to encourage problem-solving thinking, and this goal is reflected in ideas being expressed openly.

10. Lessons are designed to help the inhibited child participate via body motions, pointing, and so forth. The extremely nonverbal child should be encouraged to participate in these motions but should not be pushed, at least initially, to verbalize.

11. You may refer to situations illustrated or offered by children as *problems.* The children come to understand this word—as one youngster was heard to reveal proudly, "I solved a problem today!"

12. In addition to using the problems presented, children can make up problems or describe situations that really happened to them. The class can then offer solutions or consequences, elicited with the same techniques designed for the problem situations provided in the lessons.

13. Role-playing can be especially useful if children are able to act out the various parts in the problem situations. If the children in your class are capable of role-playing beyond that suggested by the situations included in the lessons, encourage such activity to maintain interest.

Complementary Applications

Helping children associate how they think with what they do in real-life situations is essential to the success of the program. As noted previously, suggestions are made periodically throughout the book for applying ICPS skills in the classroom—both in interpersonal situations that may arise during the day and in the curriculum. Suggestions for interaction in the classroom and curriculum ideas are given after the lesson or group of lessons to which they pertain. Presented on bordered pages, these complementary applications are just as important as the formal lessons.

Parent pages are also periodically included so parents can apply ICPS learning at home. These pages may be duplicated and shared with parents as needed. Explaining that ICPS skills are intended to help children solve everyday problems and improve or prevent behavior problems will help put the program in context.

Illustrations and Other Program Materials

The ICPS lessons make use of a number of illustrations, which immediately follow the lessons to which they pertain. You may choose to copy or even enlarge these illustrations and display them so children can see and point to them easily during the lesson, or you may place the illustrations under an opaque projector. Yet another alternative is to duplicate the illustrations and have children color and display them in the classroom to help reinforce the skills taught.

Other suggested materials are readily available in the classroom: chalkboard or easel, animal or people hand puppets, miscellaneous classroom objects (for example, crayons or blocks), and age-appropriate storybooks. In the case of hand puppets, any available can be substituted for those depicted in the lessons.

Appendix Content

Four appendixes complete this volume. Appendix A offers some guidelines for continued ICPS teaching once the formal lessons have been completed. Some questions are included to help teachers think about how they communicate key ICPS concepts to children. This appendix also includes the ICPS Teacher Self-Evaluation Checklist, intended to help teachers gauge their ability to use ICPS teaching on an ongoing basis.

Appendix B offers a summary of the steps and questions teachers ask in dialoguing child-child and teacher-child problems. These pages can be duplicated and posted in the classroom to help teachers remember to use the ICPS approach when everyday problems arise.

Appendix C provides supplementary illustrations depicting ICPS word concepts. These illustrations may be displayed on classroom walls or bulletin boards. They serve as reminders to use ICPS words on a daily basis.

Appendix D summarizes techniques the teacher can use in the formal lessons to deal with shy, nonresponsive; disruptive or obstinate; dominating; and silly behaviors.

ICPS DIALOGUING

Central to the ICPS program is the process of problem-solving dialoguing. In ICPS dialoguing, the teacher guides the child in applying ICPS concepts to solve a real-life problem. This type of dialoguing reflects a style of thought that will help children try again if their first attempt to solve a problem should fail and learn to cope with frustration when their desires must be delayed or denied.

The program materials contain many examples of dialoguing. Even very early in the program, the teacher may conduct what are called "mini-dialogues" with children. After Lessons 1 through 46 have been completed, the children will be ready for full ICPS dialogues in which they identify a problem, generate alternative solutions, explore consequences, and choose the best solution.

ICPS Dialoguing Procedures

The nature of the problem that arises will determine the exact procedures for ICPS dialoguing. In general, you will want to try to help children identify the problem, appreciate their own and others' feelings, think of solutions to the problem, and anticipate the consequences of a solution.

You will not need to memorize a set of specific questions. However, the following steps in dialoguing child-child problems and questions for resolving teacher-child conflicts will give you a sense of what is involved.

Child-child problems

STEP 1: Define the problem.

What happened? What's the matter?

That will help me understand the problem better.

STEP 2: Elicit feelings.

How do you feel?

How does _____ feel?

STEP 3: Elicit consequences.

What happened when you did that?

STEP 4: Elicit feelings about consequences.

How did you feel when _____?
(*For example:* He took your toy/she hit you)

STEP 5: Encourage the child to think of alternative solutions.

Can you think of a DIFFERENT way to solve this problem so _____?
(*For example:* You both won't be mad/she won't hit you)

STEP 6: Encourage evaluation of the solution.

> Is that a good idea or NOT a good idea?
>
> If a *good idea:* Go ahead and try that.
>
> If *not a good idea:* Oh, you'll have to think of something DIFFERENT.

STEP 7: Praise the child's act of thinking.

> *If the solution works:* Oh, you thought of that all by yourself. You're a good problem solver!
>
> *If the solution does not work:* Oh, you'll have to think of something DIFFERENT I know you're a good thinker!

Teacher-child problems

Can I talk to you AND to at the SAME time?

Is that a good place to _____?
(*For example:* Draw/leave your food)

Can you think of a good place to _____?

Is this a good time to _____?
(*For example:* Talk to your neighbor/talk to me)

When IS a good time?

How do you think I feel when you _____?
(*For example:* Don't listen/throw food/interrupt me)

Can you think of something DIFFERENT to do, until _____?
(*For example:* You can fingerpaint/I can get what you want/I can help you)

Once children become accustomed to ICPS dialoguing. most can respond to a considerably shortened version of questioning. For instance, just asking, "Can you think of a DIFFERENT idea?" is often enough to cue children that they need to apply their problem-solving skills.

Basic Principles of ICPS Dialoguing

Five basic principles, applicable to children as young as age 4, underlie the dialoguing process. The only prerequisite is that children understand the basic word concepts used by the adult. Relatively consistent application of these principles in time helps children associate their newly acquired thinking skills with what they do and how they behave.

First, both child and teacher must identify the problem. Casually saying, "What happened?"; "What's the matter? or "Tell me about it" not only helps the child clarify the problem but also ensures that you will not jump to a faulty conclusion about what is going on. For example: "Oh, now I see what the *problem* is. I thought you were mad because your friend took your truck. Now I see it's because she played with it too long and won't give it back." Discovering the child's view of the problem starts the dialoguing process on the proper course.

Second, when dialoguing, it is important to understand and deal with the real problem. The child in the preceding example thinks he has already shared his truck with his friend, but the teacher may see this child grab the truck and erroneously assume that grabbing is the problem. Actually, grabbing is the child's *solution* to the problem of getting his truck back, not the problem itself. The real problem is that the child wants his truck back.

Third, once the real problem has been identified, the teacher must not alter it to fit his or her own needs. Suppose that the teacher becomes intention showing the child in the example how to share his toys. Because the child is thinking only about how to get back a toy he knows he has already shared, the teacher's guidance will likely lead to resistance. In this case, attempting to teach the "right" thing to do may backfire.

Fourth, the child, not the teacher, must solve *the problem.* If the child is to develop the habit of thinking of his own solutions to problems and considering the potential consequences of his actions, he must be encouraged to think for himself. More than simply "listening" to the child, the teacher must actively draw out what the child thinks caused the problem, how he and others feel about the situation, his ideas about how to solve the difficulty, and what he thinks might happen if he were to put those ideas into action. In highlighting the child's thinking, the teacher does not offer solutions to the problem or suggest what might happen next. When not bombarded with "don'ts" or offered a stream of suggestions about "do's," the child is freed to think through the problem and decide for himself what and what not to do. The teacher only asks questions and, through these, guides and encourages the emergence of problem-solving thinking.

Finally, the focus is on how *the child thinks, not on* what *he thinks (in other words, the specific conclusions he comes to).* Research on the ICPS program suggests that the process of a child's thinking is more important in the long run than the content of a specific solution. Attention is therefore focused on developing a style of thinking that will help the child deal with interpersonal problems in general, not on solving the immediate problem to the teacher's satisfaction (although this often occurs). Praising a solution may inhibit further thought about other ideas. Criticizing a solution may inhibit the child's speaking freely about what is on his mind. In either case, the child's thinking will shift from generating options, consequences, and causes to selecting the one thing that meets with teacher approval. In applying these principles, the teacher transmits to the child the value judgment that *thinking* is important, and the child learns that thinking meets with adult approval.

When Not to Dialogue

It is not possible or even necessary to dialogue every problem that comes up. In fact, there are times when dialoguing is not effective and its use is better postponed. Clearly, if a child has been or is likely to be physically harmed, your first priority is to help by removing the child from danger.

In addition, sometimes a crying child just needs to cry—an angry child just needs to be angry. For example, Shelly, a super problem solver and socially competent child, was really bawling one day while fighting with LaTanya over some clay. When asked what was wrong, Shelly replied, "She (LaTanya) never shares. I always share with her!" The teacher did not dialogue with Shelly at this time. She recognized that Shelly was justifiably upset and would be able to problem solve by herself when she calmed down. In fact, she did just that.

Finally, just because your goal is to dialogue problem situations, this does not mean that you must never become angry yourself. Although angry displays should of course not be the predominant way in which you solve problems with or between children, anger is an emotion with which children must learn to cope, and your showing it occasionally is natural.

ICPS RESEARCH SUMMARY

Children were studied over a two-year period (Shure & Spivack, 1982).* In the nursery year, 113 African American inner-city children (47 boys, 66 girls) were trained, while 106 (50 boys, 56 girls) served as controls. In kindergarten, 69 trained children were still available, 39 of whom would receive training both years (15 boys, 24 girls), and 30 (12 boys, 18 girls) who would receive no further training (to test for holding power). Of the 62 still-available nursery controls, 35 (15 boys, 20 girls) were first trained in kindergarten, and 27 (12 boys, 15 girls) would constitute the never-trained controls. All four groups were initially comparable in age, sex distribution, Binet IQ (range 70-147), and teacher-rated behavioral characteristics.

- Prior to preschool (in the Fall), 36% of the children to be trained were rated as behaviorally *adjusted* (not impulsive or inhibited), and 47% of the controls were rated as adjusted. Following the intervention in the Spring, 71% of the trained children were rated as adjusted, compared to only 54% of the controls.

- Of the 44 trained children rated as *impulsive* prior to the intervention and 39 controls, 50% of the trained children became adjusted compared to only 31% of the controls.

- Of the 28 initially *inhibited* trained children and 17 controls, 75% became adjusted, compared to only 35% of the controls.

- Of the 35 initially *adjusted* children first trained in kindergarten and the 27 controls, 83% of those trained were adjusted following training, compared to only 30% of the controls. Of the 20 trained children initially showing *either impulsive or inhibited* behaviors and 16 controls, 70% were rated as adjusted in the Spring, compared to only 6% of the controls.

- At a six-month follow-up, 71% of the 80 still-remaining children who were adjusted at the end of preschool remained adjusted, compared to 42% of the 65 comparable controls, and one full year later, with 30 trained and 27 nontrained children, 77% of the trained children retained their adjusted behaviors vs. only 30% of the controls.

---

* Shure, M. B., & Spivack, G. (1982). Interpersonal problem-solving in young children: A cognitive approach to prevention. *American Journal of Community Psychology, 10*(3), 341-356.

These findings suggest the value of teaching children how to think as a way to guide behavior rather than focusing directly on behavior itself. Furthermore, the gains were not explained by initial IQ or IQ change. Linkages were stronger for solution than for consequential thinking in both the preschool and kindergarten, but consequential thinking linked more strongly in the kindergarten than in the nursery. Perhaps thinking simultaneously of what to do (now) and what might happen (later) is developmentally more possible at age five than at age four. The results also suggest that if training was not conducted in nursery, kindergarten was not too late. The percentage of adjusted controls tending to decrease by the end of the two-year period suggests the possibility that the impact of the ICPS intervention can reverse that trend.

Significance of ICPS Research

Impulsivity consists of aggression and the inability to delay gratification and cope with frustration, which are significant predictors of later, more serious problems such as violence (a form of hurting others) and substance abuse (a form of hurting oneself). Inhibition consists of the inability to stand up for one's rights and timidity and fear of other children, which are significant predictors of later depression and other forms of mental health dysfunction. ICPS intervention can provide children with skills to think about how to solve problems when they are very young, thus reducing and preventing these early high-risk behaviors in ways that will increase their chance of success and social competence in later years.

This research was conducted with low-income, primarily African American populations and funded by the Applied Research Branch and the Prevention Research Branch, National Institute of Mental Health. Research by others nationwide has now replicated the impact of ICPS on a diversity of lower- and middle-income groups, including Caucasian, Hispanic, Asian, and Native American children, as well as with special needs groups, including ADHD and Asperger's Disorder.

For information about additional research by Myrna B. Shure and George Spivack, as well as by others, contact:

Myrna B. Shure, Ph.D.
Drexel University MS 626
245 N. 15th St.
Philadelphia, PA 19102

Phone: (215) 762-7205
Fax: (215) 762-8625
Email: mshure@drexel.edu

Pre-Problem-Solving Skills

Teacher Script

Each day, for a little while, we're going to play some games called ICPS. ICPS, for us, means I Can Problem Solve. We're going to start with games that will help you think of lots of things to do when you and other children have a *problem*—like when one child wants another child or a teacher to do something, or when someone feels mad about something, or when someone has to wait for something he or she wants.

Even if you're already really good at this, you can still get better. And children who can solve problems can feel proud to say, "I'm an ICPS kid because I Can Problem Solve."

You'll get the idea of the games as we go along. Today we're going to play a game about the word IS. This word will help you solve problems later. Are you ready for the first game?

Proceed to Lesson 1.

Is

PURPOSE

To present this word concept so that children will later be sensitive to how another IS feeling, to what another IS doing, and to whether a problem solution IS a good idea

MATERIALS

None

TEACHER SCRIPT

Today we're going to start our ICPS games.

What does ICPS mean? Yes, I Can Problem Solve.

We're going to start our ICPS games with some words.

Today's ICPS word is the word IS. Are you ready?

_____ IS a boy. IS _____ a boy?

Yes, _____ IS a boy.

Repeat in quick tempo with other children in the group.

OK. Now watch me carefully. I'm going to point to someone.

If I point to a girl, raise your hand like this. *(Demonstrate.)*

What are we going to do if I point to a girl?

Right, we raise our hands. *(Go through motion again.)*

If I point to a boy, tap your knee like this. *(Demonstrate.)*

What are we going to do if I point to a boy?

Right, tap our knees. *(Go through motion again.)*

OK, now watch. *(Point to a boy and say his name.)*

Good, we tapped our knees because _____ IS a boy.

Point to each child in the group and call his or her name. Continue only as long as the group shows interest, even if only for 5 or 10 minutes.

HINT

Emphasize the ICPS words shown in capital letters with your voice in this and other lessons. If a child is teasing by responding with the opposite answer (for instance, raising a hand when Johnny's name is called), just say, "I know you're tricking me." Don't make an issue of it.

Some-All

PURPOSE

To help children distinguish between these two concepts so that they may later see that a problem solution may satisfy SOME but not ALL people

MATERIALS

None

TEACHER SCRIPT

Today's ICPS words are SOME and ALL.

Remember when we pointed to one child who IS a boy and one child who IS a girl?

Today, we're going to point to SOME boys and to SOME girls.

Are you ready? Watch me carefully.

(Boy 1) and (Boy 2) are SOME boys.

Are (Boy 1) and (Boy 2) SOME boys?

Yes *(nod head),* (Boy 1) and (Boy 2) are SOME boys.

Repeat in quick tempo with each child in the group—always in pairs.

Now watch me carefully. I am going to point to SOME boys and to SOME girls.

If I point to SOME girls, raise your hand like this. *(Demonstrate.)*

What are we going to do if I point to SOME girls?

Right, raise our hands like this.

If I point to SOME boys, tap your knee, like this.

What are we going to do if I point to SOME boys?

Right, tap our knees like this.

OK, now watch.

(Boy 3) and (Boy 4). *(Point to the boys as you say their names.)*

Good, we tapped our knees because (Boy 3) and (Boy 4) are SOME boys.

(Girl 1) and (Girl 2). *(Point to the girls as you say their names.)*

Good, we raised our hands because (Girl 1) and (Girl 2) are SOME girls.

Repeat with one or two more pairs.

Now we're going to talk about a new word. The word is ALL.

I'm going to point to ALL the boys. *(Name each boy as you point.)*

Now I'm going to point to ALL the girls. *(Name each girl as you point.)*

(Point to some boys.) Am I pointing to ALL of the boys? No. I'm pointing to SOME of the boys.

(Point to all the girls.) Am I pointing to SOME of the girls?

No, I'm pointing to ALL of the girls.

Now listen carefully. This is going to be hard.

If I point to SOME boys, tap your knee one time. *(Demonstrate.)*

If I point to ALL the boys, tap your knee two times. *(Demonstrate.)*

(Point to some boys, naming each one.) Good, we tapped our knees one time because I pointed to SOME boys.

(Point to all the boys, naming each one.) Good, we tapped our knees two times because I pointed to ALL of the boys.

If I point to SOME girls, raise your hand one time. *(Demonstrate.)*

If I point to ALL the girls, raise your hand two times. *(Demonstrate.)*

(Point to some girls, naming each one.) Good, we raised our hands one time because I pointed to SOME girls.

(Point to all the girls, naming each one.) Good, we raised our hands two times because I pointed to ALL of the girls.

Alternate pointing to some boys, all girls, and so on.

HINT

Encourage the shy nonresponder to raise hand or tap knee together with you, then shake the child's hand to reinforce this action. For a summary of suggestions for working with this and other "difficult" behaviors, see Appendix C.

Not

PURPOSE

To help children in later thinking, "This IS a good idea, that is NOT a good idea"

MATERIALS

None

TEACHER SCRIPT

Today's ICPS word is the word NOT. Listen carefully.

This IS a floor. *(Point.)* It is NOT a ceiling.

This IS my arm. This is NOT my _____. *(Let children answer.)*

This is _____'s shoe. *(Point.)* It is NOT (his/her) _____.

Repeat with other children's possessions, clothing, or body parts.

(Child 1) IS a boy. He is NOT a _____.

(Child 2) IS a boy. He is NOT a _____. *(Repeat the last response—for example, "He is NOT a girl.")*

What else is (Child 2) NOT? You can be silly and have fun.

If children do not respond, you might say, "He is NOT a balloon. He is NOT a _____." Repeat with as many children as time and interest permit.

HINT

The shy nonresponder may parrot what other children say. It is generally best not to push for another response yet. Simply say, "Good, you told us, too." In this way, the child is reinforced for saying something.

Or

PURPOSE

To show children that there is more than one way to think about things: "I can do this OR I can do that"

MATERIALS

Various classroom objects (for example, dolls, paintbrushes, toy animals)

TEACHER SCRIPT

Today we have a new ICPS word. Who can tell me what ICPS means?

Right—I Can Problem Solve.

Today's ICPS word is the word OR.

(Point to Child 1.) Am I pointing to (Child 2)?

No, I am NOT pointing to (Child 2).

(Point to Child 1.) Am I pointing to (Child 1)?

Yes, I am pointing to (Child 1).

(Point to Child 1.) Am I pointing to (Child 1) OR am I pointing to (Child 2)?

Repeat with a few other pairs.

Now close your eyes.

Pass out classroom objects to some of the children.

Now open your eyes.

Who is NOT holding something?

Who IS holding a (for example, doll)?

Who is NOT holding a (cow)?

Is _____ holding a (doll) OR a (horse)?

(Child 1), is (Child 2) holding a (doll) OR a (paintbrush)?

Alternate questions about what someone is and is not holding, ask whether someone is or is not holding something, and so forth. Let children not holding something switch with those who are.

HINT

If children stand up or walk around during the lesson, just refer to whatever they are doing. For instance, you might say, "Is Gail walking OR sitting?" Rather than insisting that the child sit down, make her actions part of the game.

And

PURPOSE

To help children see that there is more than one way to think about things, leading to later development of problem-solving ideas: "I can do this AND that"

MATERIALS

Illustration 1

TEACHER SCRIPT

Today we have a new ICPS word. The word is AND.

(Child 1), I just said your name.

(Child 2), I just said your name, too.

I just said two names: (Child 1) AND (Child 2).

Invite a third child to be the leader and call on two more children.

(Child 3) just called on (Child 4) AND (Child 5).

(Child 4), point to the floor.

Good. Now point to the chair.

Good. (Child 4) pointed to the floor AND to the _____.
(Let children respond.)

(Child 5) is wearing a (for example, blue shirt).

(Child 5) is wearing a (blue shirt) AND a _____.

AND what else is (Child 5) wearing?

Good. (Child 5) is wearing a (blue shirt) AND a _____ AND a _____.

Show children Illustration 1. You may copy or enlarge the illustration and display it so children can see and point to it easily during the lesson. Alternatively, you may place the illustration under an opaque projector or give each child a copy to hold.

This is a picture of a clown. He is wearing a hat. What else can you say about this clown?

Always repeat what the child says and all responses said thus far. For example, you might say, "He is a clown AND he is wearing a hat AND he is talking to children AND his hands are up in the air." Elicit responses about other aspects of the clown as needed. To help motivate the children, raise your arms like an orchestra leader and shout the word AND. Encourage the group to shout the word with you.

HINT

You may wish to review other ICPS words at this point. For example:

- This clown is NOT walking.
- Is this a clown OR a police officer?
- Is this clown talking to children OR to a dog?

ILLUSTRATION 1   Lesson 5

Same-Different

PURPOSE

To help children later recognize that there are DIFFERENT ways to solve the SAME problem

MATERIALS

None

TEACHER SCRIPT

Today we're going to learn two *(show two fingers)* new ICPS words. The words are SAME and DIFFERENT. Watch carefully.

I'm raising my hand. *(Raise, then lower hand.)*

Now I raise my hand again.

I just did the SAME thing. I raised my hand.

Now I'm going to do something DIFFERENT. I'm going to tap my knee. *(Tap knee.)*

See, tapping my knee *(keep tapping)*, is DIFFERENT from raising my hand. *(Raise hand.)*

Is tapping my knee *(tap knee)* DIFFERENT from raising my hand? *(Raise hand.)*

Yes, they are DIFFERENT. Tapping my knee is NOT the SAME as raising my hand.

I am stamping my foot. *(Stamp foot.)* Can you ALL do the SAME thing?

Good, we are ALL doing the SAME thing. *(If needed to encourage participation:* SOME of us are stamping our feet. Who is doing something DIFFERENT?)

Now I'm rolling my arms. Who can do something that is NOT the SAME as rolling your arms?

Good. That is NOT the SAME as rolling your arms.

It IS _____. *(If needed:* The SAME or DIFFERENT?)

Call on a couple of other children to think of a different action. After they have done so, call on a child to come up and be the leader.

_____, think of something you can do with your body.
(If needed, whisper two choices in the child's ear.)

Who can do the SAME thing _____ just did?

Who can think of something DIFFERENT? You know, something that's NOT the SAME.

Continue as long as time and interest permit.

HINT

If a child is disruptive and unwilling to participate, try to bring him into the game by noting whatever he is doing. For example, you might say, "Patrick is walking around. We are jumping. Is Patrick doing the SAME thing as we are OR something DIFFERENT?" The child will likely respond with a cheerful, "I'm doing the SAME thing. I'm jumping, too." Now the child has returned to the lesson feeling good about it.

Shy nonresponders may not yet feel comfortable talking. Some do, however, take delight in coming up front and putting their hands on their heads or performing other actions. If so, you might reinforce the child's participation by saying, "Let's ALL do the SAME thing as _____."

More Same-Different

PURPOSE

To learn the words SAME and DIFFERENT in more than one context

MATERIALS

Various classroom objects—some should be duplicates (for example, small blocks, erasers, chalk or crayons of the same colors)

TEACHER SCRIPT

Now we're going to play a DIFFERENT game with the words SAME and DIFFERENT. Close your eyes.

Place an object in each child's hand, or, if the group is large, in some children's hands.

Now open your eyes. What is (Child 1) holding?

What is (Child 2) holding?

Are (Child 1) and (Child 2) holding the SAME thing or something DIFFERENT?

What is (Child 3) holding?

Who is holding the SAME thing as (Child 3)?

What is (Child 4) holding?

Who is NOT holding the SAME thing as (Child 4)?

Is (Child 5) holding something that is the SAME as (Child 6) or something DIFFERENT?

A more advanced technique would be to give a child a crayon of one color and another child a crayon of a different color, then ask the following questions:

(Child 7) has something in (his/her) hand.

(Child 8) has something in (his/her) hand.

How are they the SAME? *(Both are crayons.)*

How are they DIFFERENT? *(They are different colors.)*

If the group is large and some children are not holding anything, ask, "Who is NOT holding something?" If desired, let individual children take turns being the leader. If the leader is incapable of asking the group questions, ask him or her to call on a child, then ask the questions yourself.

HINT

If a child walks away from the group but is within earshot, use ICPS concepts to try to bring her back: "Is Sarah holding a block OR walking away from us?" This technique is also helpful for other kinds of disruptive behavior.

Guess What?

PURPOSE

To encourage beginning deductive reasoning with ICPS words

MATERIALS

None

TEACHER SCRIPT

Ask two girls wearing skirts to stand up.

> (Child 1), stand up. (Child 2), stand up.
>
> (Child 1) AND (Child 2) are both girls.
>
> What else about them is the SAME? (*If needed:* They are both wearing skirts.)
>
> OK, you two can sit down now.
>
> Now we're going to play a guessing game.
>
> I'm going to tell two (*show two fingers*) children to stand up who have something about them that is the SAME.
>
> You try to guess what it is, OK?

Pick one boy and one girl who have on (for example, sweaters).

> What is the SAME about (Child 3) AND (Child 4)? (*If needed:* Are Child 3 AND Child 4 both wearing swimming suits? No? What is the SAME?)

Let children respond. Continue until someone says (sweater). However, if someone gives a correct response other than the one you had in mind, accept it and praise the child for good thinking. Then ask what else is the same. Repeat the exercise with other similarities. For example:

- Both boys or girls.
- Both wearing the same color.
- Both wearing glasses, earrings, sneakers, and so forth.
- Both having the same first or last name.

HINT

Ask guiding questions as necessary. For instance, if the item that is the same is earrings, you might ask, "Are they both wearing ice skates on their ears?" Be silly and have fun.

Review of ICPS Words

PURPOSE

To strengthen understanding of ICPS words

MATERIALS

None

TEACHER SCRIPT

Today we're going to play a game with ALL of our ICPS words.

Now listen carefully: (Child 1, 3, and 5), put your hands on your waists, like this. *(Demonstrate.)*

(Child 2, 4, and 6), put your hands on your shoulders, like this. *(Demonstrate.)*

If there are more than six children in the group, have the remaining ones answer the questions, with the first six children standing in front.

Do ALL the children have their hands on their waists? (*If needed:* Do SOME or ALL of the children have their hands on their waists?)

Do SOME or ALL of the children have their hands on their shoulders?

Who does NOT have hands on shoulders?

Does (Child 1) have hands on (his/her) waist OR shoulders?

Who has hands on his or her head?

Oh, I tried to trick you. Good. No one.

Who has hands on waists? _____ AND _____ AND _____.

Who does NOT have hands on waists? _____ AND _____ AND _____.

Do (Child 1) AND (Child 3) have their hands on the SAME place OR on a DIFFERENT place?

Yes, they both have their hands on their waists.

Who else has hands on the SAME place?

Yes, (Child 5).

Who has hands on a DIFFERENT place?

Who else has hands on a DIFFERENT place?

Now here's a really hard question. Listen carefully.

Look at (Child 1). Who does NOT have hands on a DIFFERENT place as (Child 1)?

Look at (Child 2). Who does NOT have hands on a DIFFERENT place as (Child 2)?

Next have children show their understanding of the ICPS words by asking them the following questions:

(Child 1), show me SOME of the tables in this room. You can walk to them and point.

(Child 2), show me ALL of the tables in this room.

(Child 3), show me something that is the SAME as this (for example, a piece of chalk).

(Child 4), show me something that is DIFFERENT from this (for example, an eraser).

(Child 5), show me something that is NOT a shoe.

(Child 6), show me a shoe OR a sock, but NOT a dress.

If there are only six children in the group, return to Child 1.

(Child 7), tell us the names of ALL of the boys in this group.

(Child 8), tell us the names of ALL of the girls in this group.

(If children know colors) (Child 9), (Child 1) is wearing (for example, red). Who else has on the SAME color?

(Child 10), who has on the SAME color as (Child 2)? Tell me two children who have on the SAME color. Who is NOT wearing that color today?

Next challenge children's understanding of the words by attempting to trick them.

(If it is a sunny day) It IS raining outside. Oh, I tried to trick you. It is NOT raining. It IS _____.

(If it is a rainy day) It IS sunny outside. *(Repeat as for sunny day.)*

HINT

If in the first part of this lesson a child takes his hands off his waist or shoulders, just say, for example, "Oh, Mark put his hands at his side. Are his hands in the SAME place as (Child 1's) OR in a DIFFERENT place?" This helps bring the child back into the game by using ICPS concepts.

More Review of ICPS Words

PURPOSE

To further strengthen understanding of ICPS words

MATERIALS

Illustration 2

TEACHER SCRIPT

Today we're going to play a new game with our ICPS words.

Show children Illustration 2.

What is happening in this picture?

Is this boy *(point to any boy)* standing OR is he sitting down?

(Very dramatically, point to some children.) Are these SOME children OR are these ALL of the children in this picture?

Good, these are SOME children.

This boy *(point)* IS standing. Show me a child who is NOT standing.

This boy *(point)* IS blowing his horn. This girl *(point)* IS blowing her horn, too.

Are these children doing the SAME thing OR something DIFFERENT?

Yes, they are doing the SAME thing.

Now show me someone who is NOT blowing a horn.

This girl *(point to standing girl)* IS blowing a horn.

She is blowing a horn AND she is _____. *(Let children respond.)*

What else is she doing?

How are these two girls *(point)* the SAME?

Yes, they are both blowing horns.

How are they DIFFERENT?

Yes, one is standing and one is sitting.

Do you see anything else about them that is DIFFERENT?

Show me SOME children in this picture.

Show me ALL the children in this picture.

This boy *(point to the boy who is blowing a horn)* is NOT blowing his horn.

Oh, you caught me. I tried to trick you. He IS blowing his horn.

This boy *(point to the boy who is sitting)* is NOT sitting.

Oh, you caught me again. He IS sitting.

(Point to the boy with shorts on.) This boy IS wearing pants.

No? Oh, you caught me again. He is NOT wearing pants. He IS wearing shorts.

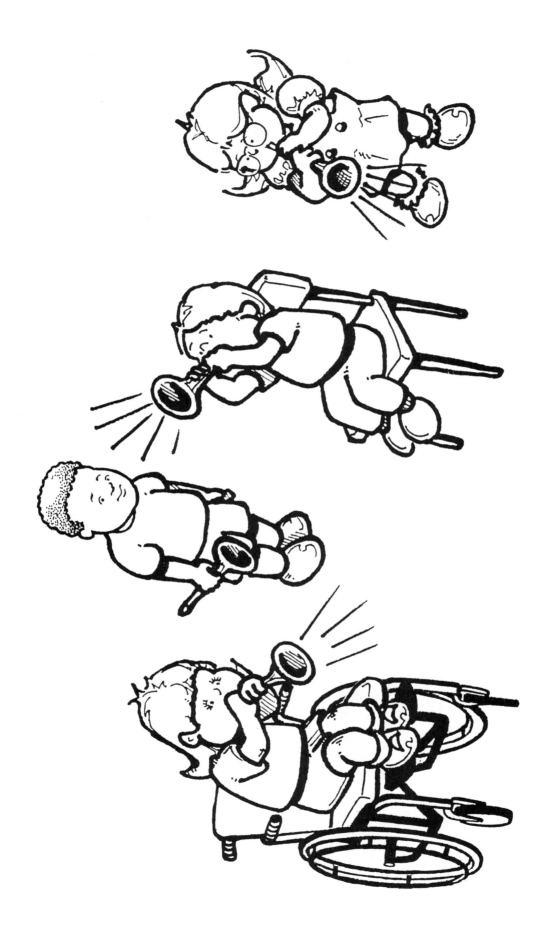

ILLUSTRATION 2 Lesson 10

ICPS Words: Is, Some-All, Not, Or, And, Same-Different

Try incorporating and building upon individual ICPS words in the classroom. This will help you later on when you use ICPS dialoguing in problem situations with children. It will also help children extend learning to real life.

JUICETIME/LUNCHTIME

Tell me one boy who IS at our table.

Tell me one girl who IS at our table.

Tell me SOME of the children at our table.

Tell me ALL of the girls at our table.

Tell me SOME of the children who have on (for example, blue tops).

Who is NOT at our table?

This IS a (potato). It is NOT a _____.

(Point to a different food.) This IS a _____. *(Name something it is not.)*

No? Oh, I tried to trick you. This IS a _____.

_____ IS a boy. He is NOT an elephant.

He is NOT a _____.

What else is he NOT?

_____, are you eating OR are you painting?

_____, are you eating (meat AND peas) OR (chicken AND rice)?

Is this (cracker) the SAME as this (juice)?

No, they are _____. *(If needed: Are they the SAME or DIFFERENT?)*

Who likes (chicken)?

Who likes something DIFFERENT?

Is it OK for DIFFERENT children to like DIFFERENT things?

Yes, it is OK.

_____ likes (chicken). Who likes the SAME thing as _____?

TRANSITIONS

(Child 1) IS helping to put the blocks away.

IS (Child 2) helping, too?

No, she is NOT helping.

We are getting ready to wash up for lunch.

Are we ALL getting ready to wash up for lunch?

No, _____ is doing something DIFFERENT.

What do we do to get ready for lunch?

Yes, we put our toys away AND go to the bathroom.

Did _____ put his toys away AND go to the bathroom?

Is _____ getting ready to go outside OR is she fussing?

Are SOME of you getting ready to go outside OR are ALL of
you ready?

FREE PLAY

What IS _____ doing?

Who is NOT doing what _____ IS doing?

_____ IS building an airport.

No? I tried to trick you. What IS she doing?

Tell me SOME of the children who are in the sandbox.

Tell me ALL of the children who are in the sandbox.

Tell me SOME children who are NOT in the sandbox.

Are (Child 1) AND (Child 2) on the slide OR are (Child 1) AND
(Child 3) on the slide?

_____ is coloring with a (red) crayon. Who is coloring with the
SAME color as _____?

Who is coloring with a DIFFERENT color?

IS _____ painting?

Who is doing the SAME thing as _____?

LISTENING/NOT LISTENING

(Child 1) IS listening. (Child 2) is NOT listening. He is doing
something DIFFERENT.

Is (Child 2) listening OR NOT listening?

Is (Child 1) or (Child 2) listening?

Are SOME of you listening OR are ALL of you listening?

If ALL of you talk at the SAME time, can I hear *(point to ears)* what _____ is saying?

Are you ALL going to answer OR just _____?

MINI-DIALOGUES

The following examples show how a teacher uses the ICPS word DIFFERENT in two problem situations.

Situation 1: Ben grabs a toy truck from Celia.

Teacher: *(To Ben)* What happened? What's the matter?

Ben: She's had it already.

Teacher: *(To Celia)* What do you think happened?

Celia: I'm not done making my road!

Teacher: *(To both)* It looks as though you two see what happened a DIFFERENT way. That means you have a problem. Can we solve this problem? *(To Ben)* Grabbing is *one* way to get the toy. Can you think of a DIFFERENT way? You can grab OR _____.

Ben: No! I want it now.

Teacher: Celia, can you think of a DIFFERENT idea?

Celia: He can have the tractor until I'm done with the truck.

Situation 2: Laurie is exhibiting nagging, demanding behavior.

Laurie: I want the collage stuff.

Teacher: I can't get it now—we're about to clean up for lunchtime.

Laurie: But I want it now. I won't make a mess.

Teacher: I know you won't make a mess. You can play with it right after lunch. Can you think of something DIFFERENT to do now that will be easy to put away quickly?

Laurie: No! I want the collage!

Teacher: We're going to have lunch in 5 minutes. *(Shows time on watch.)* I bet if you think hard, you can think of something to do now all by yourself.

Laurie: *(Thinks a minute.)* I'll dress the baby doll.

Had the idea to dress the baby doll been the teacher's instead of Laurie's, the child would likely have resisted and continued to nag.

YOUR IDEAS

Write down your own thoughts for applying these ICPS words in classroom interactions.

IS

_____

_____

_____

SOME-ALL

_____

_____

_____

NOT

_____

_____

_____

OR

_____

_____

_____

AND

_____

_____

_____

SAME-DIFFERENT

_____

_____

_____

ICPS Words: Is, Some-All, Not, Or, And, Same-Different

Try applying the ICPS word concepts in the following curriculum areas.

LANGUAGE ARTS: STORY COMPREHENSION

The name of the (boy/girl) in the story I just read IS _____.

(His/her) name is NOT _____.

Are ALL the children in the story (boys/girls) OR are SOME of them (boys/girls)?

What did the (boy/girl) do?

What did _____ do? *(Name another character.)*

Did the (boy/girl) AND _____ do the SAME thing OR something DIFFERENT?

LANGUAGE ARTS: ORAL COMMUNICATION

This morning we went to the (for example, zoo).

Who can tell us what we saw? *(Allow children to give several responses.)*

Did we see a zebra AND a giraffe OR a zebra AND a kitten?

We saw lots of animals. What else did we see?

We saw animals AND _____. *(If needed:* A man selling peanuts OR a man selling sweaters?)

We went to the (for example, birdhouse). What sounds did you hear the birds make?

What sounds did the birds NOT make?

LANGUAGE ARTS: VISUAL DISCRIMINATION

What's Missing?

Draw the following illustrations on chalkboard or easel, or use actual pictures if available—for example, a flower without a stem, horse without a tail, and so on.

What is NOT here? (*If needed:* What does this face have that this one—*point*—does NOT have?)

What is NOT here? (*If needed:* What does this dog have that this one—*point*—does NOT have?)

A Familiar Situation

What IS on your dinner table?

What is NOT on your dinner table? (*If needed:* A bear is NOT on your dinner table. What else is NOT on your dinner table?)

Colors

Use familiar objects such as crayons at first, then expand to other objects according to children's abilities.

This crayon IS red. IS this crayon red?

Yes, this crayon IS red.

This crayon IS blue. IS this crayon blue?

Yes, this crayon IS blue.

Which crayon is NOT red?

Which one is NOT blue?

(*Display two new colors.*) Who can show me a crayon that is NOT red and is NOT blue?

Do you know what color it IS?

Show me a red crayon AND a yellow one.

Show me a red crayon AND one that is NOT blue.

Show me a red crayon OR a blue one, but NOT a yellow one.

MATH

Numbers

Activity 1

Put the numerals 1 and 2 on chalkboard or easel, or if you have wooden or plastic numerals, hold them up or have a child hold them up. Use more numerals if the group can handle them.

This IS the number 1. IS this the number 1 OR the number 2?

This IS the number 1. It is NOT the number 3.

It is NOT the number _____.

Who knows a DIFFERENT number it is NOT?

Activity 2

Write the sequence 1–1–2–2 on chalkboard or easel, or lay plastic or wooden numerals on a table. Use more numerals according to children's abilities.

Show me two numbers that are the SAME.

Show me two numbers that are DIFFERENT.

Show me two numbers that are the SAME AND one number that is DIFFERENT.

Show me a number that is NOT a 1.

Show me a number that IS a 2.

Show me a 1 AND a 2.

Activity 3

Write the sequence 1–1–1–1–2–2–2–2 on chalkboard or easel, or lay plastic or wooden numerals on a table.

Show me ALL of the number 1s.

Show me SOME of the number 2s.

Show me ALL of the number 2s AND SOME of the number 1s.

Shapes

Activity 1

Place wooden or plastic shapes on chalkboard ledge or table. Let children hold up, or draw on chalkboard or easel.

This IS a circle. IS this a circle?

Yes, this IS a circle.

This IS a square. IS this a square?
Yes, this IS a square.

IS this a square?
No, this is NOT a square. This IS a _____.

This IS a circle.
No? Oh, I tried to trick you. This IS a _____.

_____, finish the first shape.

Now finish the next one.

Did you finish a circle AND a triangle OR a circle AND a square?
*(If children are able, add an incomplete triangle, rectangle, and
cube. Ask children to finish the drawings.)*

Activity 2

Draw the following sequence of shapes on chalkboard or easel.

Show me one circle.

Show me ALL the shapes that are the SAME as the circle.

Show me a square.

Show me ALL the squares.

Show me SOME of the circles.

Show me a circle AND a square.

Show me one square AND the rectangle.

Point to a shape that is NOT the triangle.

Shapes and Numbers

Display four red circles and two blue circles. Color them with chalk, if needed.

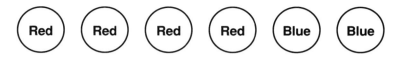

Show me ALL of the circles.

Show me ALL of the red circles.

Show me SOME of the red circles.

Show me two circles that are the SAME color.

Show me two circles that are DIFFERENT colors.

Show me two circles that are the SAME color AND one circle that is a DIFFERENT color.

Show me a circle, but NOT a red one.

Shapes and Colors

Use plastic shapes or draw shapes on chalkboard or easel. Children can respond in words or by pointing.

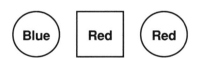

I am thinking of a circle. It is NOT red. What am I thinking of?

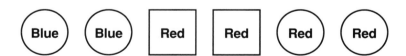

I am thinking of SOME circles. They are NOT red. What am I thinking of?

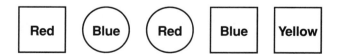

I am thinking of ALL the shapes that are NOT blue. What am I thinking of?

I am thinking of a square. It is NOT red OR blue. It IS _____.

Sets

Draw the following sets on chalkboard or easel.

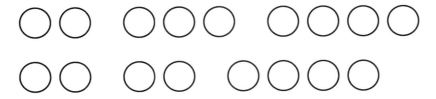

(Point to the first set.) These are 2 circles (pennies, raisins).

Show me ALL the sets of 2.

Show me SOME sets of 2.

Show me ALL the sets that are NOT 2.

Show me one set of 2 AND one set of 4.

Spatial Relationships/Comparisons

Use ICPS words to help children learn new concepts, one at a time: big/little, top/bottom, inside/outside, tall/short, round/flat, and so forth.

Is this the top of the page OR the bottom?

How are ◯ AND ◯ the SAME?

How are they DIFFERENT?

Show me something in the room that IS round.

Show me something in the room that is NOT round.

SOCIAL STUDIES

Home and Family

If your grandmother lives with you, raise your hand.

If your grandmother does NOT live with you, raise your hand.

Do ALL of you OR SOME of you live with your grandmothers?

What does your mom do that you do NOT do? (*If needed:* Do you drive the car OR does your mom do that?)

What else does your mom do that you do NOT do?

Do you have a sister?

(To another child) Do you have a sister?

Who else has a sister?

Who does NOT have a sister?

Do ALL of you have sisters?

Do SOME of you have sisters?

What do you do that your sister does NOT do? *(Repeat with brother, sister and brother, new baby, and so on.)*

Community Helpers

What does a mail carrier do?

What does a mail carrier NOT do?

What does a police officer do that a mail carrier does NOT do?

What does a nurse do?

Who puts out fires?

Does a doctor help sick people OR sell you clothes?

SCIENCE

Plants and Animals

What do our fish need to live? _____ AND _____.

What do our fish eat?

What do our plants eat?

Do fish and plants eat the SAME thing OR something DIFFERENT?

What do fish NOT eat?

What do plants NOT eat?

What do people NOT eat?

A dog has four legs. What else does a dog have?

What does a dog NOT have?

A dog goes _____. *(Imitate sound.)*

What sound does a dog NOT make? *(Repeat with other animals.)*

Textures

Use collage materials such as fur, stone, cotton, sandpaper, wool, and velvet.

Does cotton feel soft OR scratchy?

Show me something that does NOT feel soft.

Show me ALL the things that do feel soft.

Household Items

What do you get from your faucet that you do NOT get from your sock?

Do you dry yourself with a towel OR with water?

Do you cook with a stove OR with a sink?

Seasons

Does it snow in the winter OR in the summer?

What do you wear in the winter that you do NOT wear in the summer? (*If needed:* What do you wear on your hands, on your feet, and so forth.)

What do you wear in the summer that you do NOT wear in the winter?

What can you do in the summer that you can NOT do in the winter?

What can you do in the winter that you can NOT do in the summer?

Do leaves fall off the trees in the winter OR in the fall?

Time

What can you do now that you could NOT do when you were a baby?

What did you do as a baby AND you do now?

Beginning Classification

A dog has four legs. What other animal has four legs?

Do a dog AND a _____ AND a _____ have the SAME number of legs?

Can DIFFERENT animals have the SAME number of legs?

What animal does NOT have four legs?

YOUR IDEAS

Write down your own thoughts for applying these ICPS words in the curriculum.

IS

_____

_____

_____

SOME-ALL

_____

_____

_____

NOT

_____

_____

_____

OR

_____

_____

_____

AND

_____

_____

_____

SAME-DIFFERENT

_____

_____

_____

Welcome to ICPS!

What do you do when your child:

- Nags, demands, or cries?
- Hits other children or takes away their toys?
- Won't listen to you or do what you ask?

Problems are normal. We can all get better at solving them. So can your 3- or 4-year-old child. Your youngster is part of a special program at school called I Can Problem Solve. We call it ICPS.

ICPS helps your child think about:

- What to do
- Whether an idea is a good one
- What else to do

ICPS helps you think about these things, too.

How can you help? Use the ICPS words and concepts just a few minutes each day.

Happy ICPSing!

ICPS Words: Is, Not, Same-Different

These specific ICPS words will help your child eventually be able to think of an idea, decide whether it IS or is NOT a good one, then think of something DIFFERENT he or she can do. The following examples show some ways you can use these words.

AT MEALTIME

- This IS a (for example, hamburger). It is NOT a _____.
- What else is it NOT?
- Show me something that is DIFFERENT from a (hamburger).

IN THE GROCERY STORE

- This IS an (apple). It is NOT a _____.
- Show me the SAME thing.
- Show me something that is DIFFERENT.

WHILE DRESSING

- This shirt IS (blue). It is NOT (yellow).
- Bring me your (white) socks, NOT your (blue) ones.
- IS your shirt the SAME color as your pants?

  If not the same: No, it IS _____.

  If needed: SAME or DIFFERENT?

ON A BUS

- I see a (tree). What do you see?
- Did we see the SAME thing?
- Did we see something DIFFERENT?

WHILE WATCHING TELEVISION

- We are watching _____. *(Name a program you are watching.)*
- We are NOT watching _____. *(Name a program you are not watching.)*
- What else are we NOT watching?

YOUR IDEAS

ICPS Words: Or, And, Some-All

Along with the ICPS words IS, NOT, and SAME-DIFFERENT, these words will help your child be able later on to think:

- I can do this OR that.
- I can do this AND that.
- That IS a good idea SOME of the time, NOT ALL of the time.

AT MEALTIME

- Is this (for example, spinach) OR a hamburger?
- This is (spinach) AND _____. *(Point.)*
- Are the (potatoes) SOME or ALL of the food on your plate?

IN THE GROCERY STORE

- Is this an (apple) OR a peach?
- Show me an (apple) AND a (banana).
- Show me an (orange) AND a (pear), but NOT a (tomato).
- Did I buy ALL or SOME of the (paper towels) in the store?

WHILE DRESSING

- Is this a shirt OR a sock?
- Are ALL of your socks (red) OR are SOME of your socks (red)?

ON A BUS

- I see a (tree) AND a (red building). Tell me what you see.
- Did we see the SAME thing OR something DIFFERENT?

WHILE WATCHING TELEVISION

- Is this *(name program you are watching)* OR is this *(name program you are not watching)*?

YOUR IDEAS

_____

_____

_____

_____

_____

Happy

PURPOSE

To help children identify their own and others' HAPPY feelings, for later anticipation of positive and negative consequences

MATERIALS

Illustration 3

TEACHER SCRIPT

(Show a big smile.) What am I doing? *(Point to smiling mouth.)*
Yes, I am smiling. When I smile I feel HAPPY.

(Laugh, very dramatically.) Now what am I doing?
Yes, I am laughing. When I laugh I feel HAPPY.
I feel HAPPY when I laugh AND when I smile.

_____, can you show me a HAPPY face?
Good. *(To other children)* What is _____ doing?
Yes, (he/she) is laughing (or smiling).

Repeat with a couple of other children, then show children Illustration 3.

Here is a picture of a boy. What is he doing?
Yes, he is smiling (or laughing). How do you think he feels?
Yes, HAPPY. What makes you think he feels HAPPY?
Yes, he is smiling (or laughing).

When someone gives me ice cream, *I* feel HAPPY.
Tell me something DIFFERENT that makes *you* feel HAPPY.

Call on several children. If someone repeats an answer, say, "Is that the SAME thing OR something DIFFERENT? Can you tell me something DIFFERENT that makes you feel HAPPY?"

HINT

If a shy nonresponder repeats another child's response, praise by saying, "Good, you told us, too."

ILLUSTRATION 3   Lesson 11

Sad

PURPOSE

To help children identify their own and others' SAD feelings, for later anticipation of positive and negative consequences

MATERIALS

Illustration 3 (from Lesson 11) and Illustration 4 (from this lesson)

TEACHER SCRIPT

(Show a very sad face and pretend to cry.) What am I doing?

Yes, I'm crying. When I am crying or puckering my lips *(demonstrate),* I feel SAD.

How do I feel when I cry?

Yes, SAD.

_____, can you show me a SAD face?

Good. *(To other children)* What is _____ doing?

Yes, crying.

Repeat with a couple of other children, then show children Illustration 4.

Here is a picture of a girl. What is she doing?

Yes, she is crying. How do you think she feels?

Yes, SAD. What makes you think she feels SAD?

Yes, she is crying.

When people hurt themselves, I feel SAD.

Tell me something DIFFERENT that makes you feel SAD.

As in Lesson 11, ask for another response if someone repeats an answer. Again, if the child is a nonresponder, do not push, just praise for "telling us, too."

Who IS here today?

Who is NOT here today?

Repeat every now and then to review these concepts. Next show children Illustration 3.

How is this boy *(point)* feeling?

Yes, HAPPY.

Show children Illustration 4.

How is this girl *(point)* feeling?

Yes, SAD. Do this boy and this girl feel the SAME way OR a DIFFERENT way?

Yes, they feel a DIFFERENT way.

Who can look the SAME way as this girl? *(Point to Illustration 4.)*

Good, _____ and this girl look the SAME way.

Who can look DIFFERENT from this girl? *(Point.)*

Good, _____ looks HAPPY, and this girl looks SAD.

Is this girl *(point)* HAPPY?

No, she is NOT HAPPY. She feels _____.

Yes, she feels SAD.

ILLUSTRATION 4 Lesson 12

How Can We Tell: Seeing and Hearing

PURPOSE

To introduce the concept "There's more than one way," in this case with regard to finding out how someone feels

MATERIALS

A penny

A key

TEACHER SCRIPT

(Hold up the penny.) Is this a penny?

How can you tell?

You can see with your _____. *(Point dramatically to your eyes, then let children respond.)*

Now close your eyes. What is this, a pencil or a key?

You can't tell because you can't see with your eyes.

Now open your eyes.

(Hold up the key.) Now tell me what this is.

How can you tell?

You can see with your _____.

A person can be HAPPY. A person can be SAD.

(Smile dramatically.) Am I HAPPY OR am I SAD?

How can we tell?

We can tell by seeing with our eyes.

How can we tell? *(Point dramatically to your eyes.)*

By seeing with our _____.

Let's talk about our eyes some more. Show me your eyes. Point to your eyes.

We can see with our eyes. What can we do with our eyes?

Yes, we can see with our eyes.

Now close your eyes. Keep them closed.

Cover your eyes with both hands.

Can you see with your eyes now?

No, you can NOT see with your eyes when they are closed.

Now open your eyes.

Can you see with your eyes now?

Yes, you can see with your eyes when they're open.

Now let's talk about our ears.

I want you to point to your ears.

We can hear with our ears.

What can we do with our ears?

Yes, we can hear with our ears.

Can we see with our ears?

No, we can NOT see with our ears.

What can we do with our ears?

Yes, we can hear with our ears.

Can we hear with our eyes?

No, we can NOT hear with our eyes.

What can we do with our eyes?

Yes, we can see with our eyes.

I am laughing. *(Demonstrate.)* Am I HAPPY OR am I SAD?

How can you tell I'm HAPPY? (*If response is "You're laughing":* How can you tell I'm laughing?)

Did you see me with your eyes?

Did you hear me with your ears?

Yes, you can tell two ways.

One way you can tell I'm HAPPY is to see me with your eyes.

You can see I'm laughing.

Way number two you can tell I'm HAPPY is that you can hear me laughing.

You can hear me with your ears.

More How Can We Tell

PURPOSE

To strengthen the idea that there is more than one way to find out how someone feels

MATERIALS

A large book or sheet of paper

TEACHER SCRIPT

My eyes *(point to eyes)* can _____. *(Let children respond.)*

My ears *(point to ears)* can _____.

Do my eyes and ears do the SAME thing?

No, they do NOT do the SAME thing. They do DIFFERENT things.

What can my eyes do that my ears can NOT do?

Yes, my eyes can see. My ears can NOT _____.

What can my ears do that my eyes can NOT do?

Yes, my ears can hear.

My eyes can NOT _____.

Cover your face with a big book or sheet of paper and laugh dramatically.

Am I HAPPY OR am I SAD?

How can you tell?

Keep the book or paper covering your face. If response is "You're laughing," ask, "How can you tell I'm laughing?"

Can you see me?

No, you can NOT see me with your eyes.

Can you hear me with your ears?

Yes, you can hear me with your ears.

Take the book or paper away.

Now we have two *(show two fingers)* ways to find out if someone is HAPPY.

Way number one is to *(point to eyes)* see with our eyes. What's one way?

To see with our _____. *(Keep repeating, very slowly, until children say "eyes.")*

Way number two is to hear with our *(point to ears).*

Way number two is to hear with our _____. *(Keep repeating, very slowly, until children say "ears.")*

What's way number one? To see with our _____. *(Point to eyes and let children respond.)*

What's way number two? To hear with our _____. *(Point to ears and let children respond.)*

Now you know we have two ways.

Can anyone think of a third way to find out if someone is HAPPY? Way number three?

Children may respond by saying "Ask him" or some such. If so, act out this way by asking a child, "Are you HAPPY?"

HINT

If children do not suggest asking as a way of finding out or if they give an irrelevant response, just say maybe and let it go. This third way appears in the next lesson.

How Can We Tell: Asking

PURPOSE

To suggest that asking is a third way to find out how someone feels

MATERIALS

lllustrations 5–7

TEACHER SCRIPT

Show children Illustration 5.

Who can tell us what this is? *(Point to the drawing of a dog.)*

Right, a dog. Who knows what this is? *(Point to the drawing of a turtle.)*

Right, a turtle.

If you could choose a dog OR a turtle to take home for a pet—that means you can only choose one *(show one finger)*—which one would you choose, (Child 1)?

If no response, guide the child to point to the preferred animal.

(Child 2), which one would you choose? Only one.

(Child 1) chose the _____. (Child 2) chose the _____.

Did (Child 1) AND (Child 2) choose the SAME thing OR something DIFFERENT?

Yes, they chose (the SAME/a DIFFERENT) thing.

Repeat with several more pairs of children until some have expressed different preferences.

DIFFERENT children choose DIFFERENT things.

Is it OK for (Child 3) to choose something DIFFERENT from (Child 4)?

Yes, it is OK for DIFFERENT children to choose DIFFERENT things.

Show children Illustration 6.

(Child 5), would this bird make you HAPPY?

(He/she) said (yes/no). How did we find out? What did we just do?
We asked.

Let's ask (Child 6). (Child 6), would a bird make you HAPPY?

(To the group) Together, ask, "Would a bird make you HAPPY?"

What did we just do to find out if a bird makes (Child 6) HAPPY?

Yes, we asked AND we heard (him/her) tell us. We heard with
our _____. *(Point to ears.)*

(Child 7), show us the animal you would choose—the bird OR the
fish. *(Help the child point, if necessary.)*

(Child 7) chose the (bird/fish). How did we find out?

We saw (Child 7) point. We saw (him/her) with our _____. *(Point
to eyes.)*

(Child 7), tell us which one you chose. Now how did we find out?

We asked and heard (him/her) tell us. We heard him with
our _____. *(Point to ears.)*

Show children Illustration 7.

(Child 8), tell us whether you would choose the cat OR the rabbit.

Yes, I heard with my _____ *(point to ears)* AND Child 8 chose the
(cat/rabbit).

How did I find out? I _____. *(If needed:* Asked.)

Let's ask together: "(Child 8), would a (cat/rabbit) make you
HAPPY?"

Now we have three *(show three fingers)* ways to find out what makes
people HAPPY.

Number one, we can see with our _____. *(Point to eyes.)*

Number two, we can hear with our _____. *(Point to ears.)*

AND number three, we can _____. *(Point to mouth. If needed,
remind children that they can ask.)*

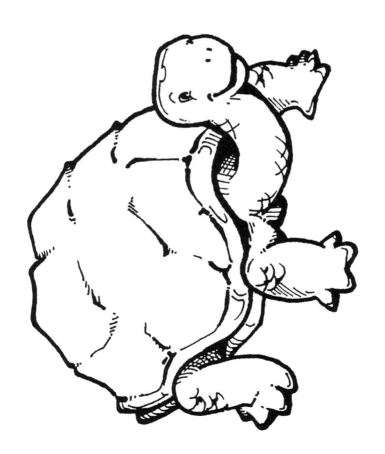

ILLUSTRATION 5   Lesson 15

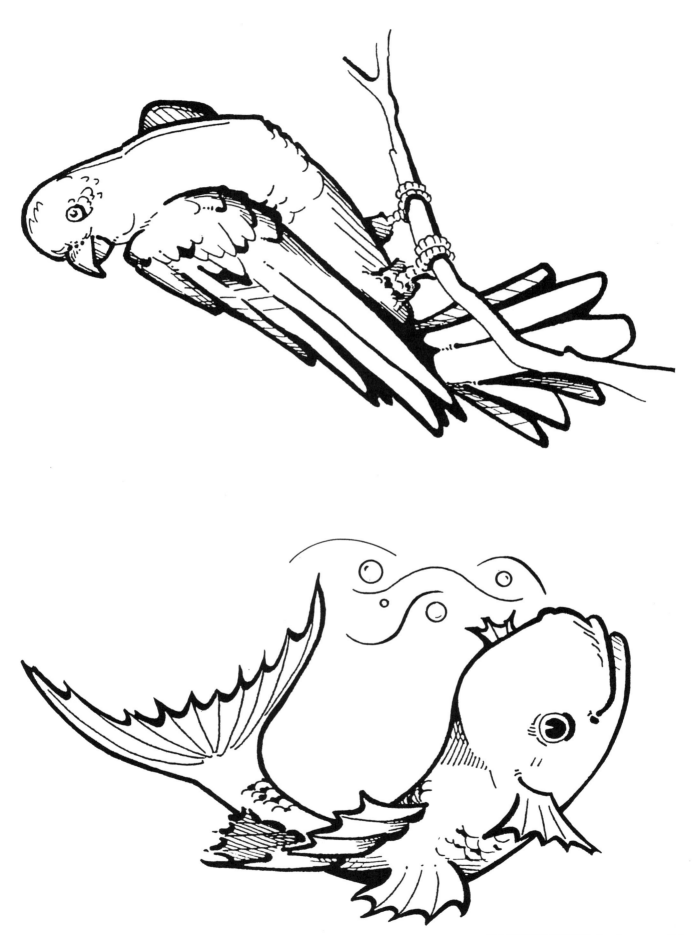

ILLUSTRATION 6 Lesson 15

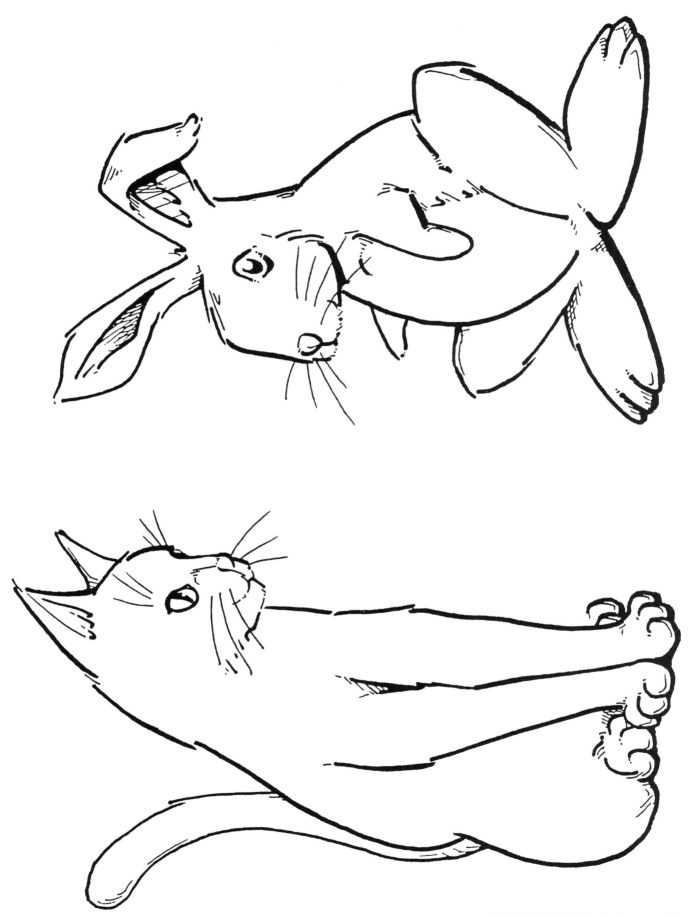

ILLUSTRATION 7 Lesson 15

Can I Make You Happy?

PURPOSE

To help children think about how to influence the feelings of others

MATERIALS

None

TEACHER SCRIPT

Today's ICPS game is about how we can make someone HAPPY.

Let's see. How about (Child 1)? How can we make (him/her) HAPPY?

Anyone have an idea?

Allow children to respond.

Maybe that would make (him/her) HAPPY. Maybe that would NOT. How can we find out?

Yes, let's ask.

(Child 1), would a _____ make you HAPPY?

If yes: That's one way to make (Child 1) HAPPY. Let's think of a DIFFERENT way to make (him/her) HAPPY—way number two. *(Show two fingers.)*

If no: Oh, that would NOT make (Child 1) HAPPY. We'll have to think of something DIFFERENT.

Repeat until the group comes up with two or three things that make the first child happy, then ask a new child. Repeat with four or five children or as interest permits.

HINT

You may wish to emphasize the concepts as the following example shows.

A doll makes Taylor HAPPY. Jason, does a doll make you HAPPY?

Do Taylor and Jason like the SAME thing OR something DIFFERENT?

If same: DIFFERENT children can like the SAME thing.

If different: DIFFERENT children can like DIFFERENT things.

Also: Taylor likes dolls AND airplanes. The SAME child can like DIFFERENT things.

Angry

PURPOSE

To help children identify their own and others' ANGRY feelings, for later anticipation of positive and negative consequences

MATERIALS

Illustration 8

TEACHER SCRIPT

Show me a HAPPY face.

Good, now show me a SAD face.

Good, now watch me. *(Frown dramatically.)* What am I doing? Who knows how I feel now?

I am frowning. I feel ANGRY when I frown. Feeling ANGRY is the same as feeling mad.

If someone takes something from me and does NOT ask first, I feel ANGRY.

Now we have three *(show three fingers)* ways people can feel.

People can feel HAPPY. *(Show happy face.)* That's way number one.

People can feel SAD. *(Show sad face.)* That's way number two.

People can feel ANGRY. *(Show angry face.)* That's way number three.

Show children Illustration 8.

Here is a picture of a boy. How do you think he feels?

How can you tell? (*If the response is "He's frowning":* How can you tell he is frowning?)

You can see him with your _____.

OK, now listen carefully. (Child 1), do cookies make you HAPPY? (*If no:* What makes you HAPPY?)

If (Child 2) let (Child 1) have a (cookie), how would (Child 1) feel?

Yes, HAPPY. How might (Child 1) feel if (Child 2) would NOT let (him/her) have a (cookie)?

Maybe SAD or maybe ANGRY.

Now let's pretend (Child 1) has a cookie and (Child 3) snatches it—grabs it right out of (his/her) hand and eats it.

How might that make (Child 1) feel?

How can we find out?

Let's ask (him/her). Who would like to ask?

Allow children to ask for and listen to responses. Repeat the entire questioning process with several children. Ask if one child's response is the same or different from another's to help review these concepts.

ILLUSTRATION 8   Lesson 17

Let's Pretend

PURPOSE

To help children further identify HAPPY, SAD, and ANGRY feelings

MATERIALS

Various small classroom objects (for example, crayons, erasers, blocks)

TEACHER SCRIPT

Now let's pretend.

Instruct one child to grab an object from another child.

Remember, this is just a game.

(To Child 1, whose object was grabbed) How do you feel about that?

(To Child 2) Now, give it back to (him/her).

(To Child 1) How do you feel now?

Repeat with a couple more children.

Now let's pretend that (Child 3) lost (his/her) dog.

(Child 3), can you look SAD? *(If necessary, help the child with the proper expression.)*

(To the group) How does (Child 3) feel?

Yes, _____. *(If needed:* SAD.)

How would (Child 3) feel if (his/her) dog came home again? *(If needed:* HAPPY.)

Now let's pretend (Child 4) found (Child 3's) dog but wouldn't give it back.

How might (Child 3) feel?

Let's find out. How can we find out? *(Encourage children to ask.)*

Let's pretend next that it's really cold outside and (Child 5) doesn't have any mittens.

If (he/she) took yours *(point to Child 6),* how would you feel?

(Child 7), what would make you ANGRY?

If no response, suggest a possible situation. For example:

- You weren't invited to a birthday party.
- Someone broke your milk glass.
- Someone broke your cookie and ate it.
- Someone scribbled on your painting.

HINT

Some children become more upset than usual while discussing their emotions. However, such discomfort is only temporary. Once children can think through their emotions, most can cope with them better than before. If a child does become upset during this or any lesson to follow, try encouraging the other children to think of ways to make her feel happy. They can ask, "Do you like _____?" as will be illustrated in Lesson 29. Soon the child will smile and rejoin the game.

What Am I Doing?
What Do I Want You to Do?

PURPOSE

To encourage listening and paying attention, needed to find out what others are thinking and feeling

MATERIALS

None

TEACHER SCRIPT

Watch and listen very carefully.

Today's ICPS game is called What Am I Doing? What Do I Want You To Do?

(Point to your eyes.) I am pointing to my ears.

No? I am pointing to my _____. *(Let children respond.)*

(Point to your ears with one hand and to your knee with the other hand.) I am pointing to my toes AND to my elbow.

No? I am pointing to my _____ AND to my _____.

(Stamp your foot and raise your arm at the same time, then return to a neutral position.) Did I clap my hands AND scream?

Who can show me what I did do?

Yes, I stamped my foot AND raised my arm at the SAME time.

(Stamp your foot, raise your arm, and rub your tummy at the same time, then return to a neutral position.) Who can show me ALL the things I just did?

Yes, I stamped my foot, raised my arm, AND rubbed my tummy at the SAME time.

OK, now watch. First this *(stamp your foot)*. Then this *(jump)*.
And next *(hop)*.

Who can show me ALL the things I just did?

Can you stamp your foot AND hop at the SAME time?

No, you can NOT stamp your foot AND hop at the SAME time.

We just played the game What Am I Doing?

Now we're going to change the game to What Do I Want You to Do?

First, I'll help you.

(Child 1), point to the ceiling.

Good, now point to the floor.

Good, now clap your hands.

Who can do ALL the things (Child 1) just did?

Do with a few children, increasing the number of activities as your group can handle.

Now I need a leader.

(Child 2), come up here and do two *(show two fingers)* things.
(If necessary, whisper ideas into the child's ear.)

Who can do what (Child 2) just did?

Repeat with a few more children, as time and interest permit.

A Story

PURPOSE

To strengthen story comprehension and use of ICPS words, as well as to help children understand feelings from more than one point of view

MATERIALS

Any storybook

TEACHER SCRIPT

Read any storybook to the class, then reread and, at appropriate points, ask the following questions:

Is _____ a _____? *(Name a character in the story and describe something he or she is not—for example, a 6-year-old.)*

No, (he/she) is NOT a _____. (He/she) IS a _____.

Did the person _____ or did (he/she) _____? *(Describe something the character did not do, then something he or she did do.)*

How do you think the person felt when _____? *(Describe a particular event.)*

Why do you think she felt that way?

Would you feel the SAME way OR a DIFFERENT way as the person about that? *(If the response is "different," let the child discuss feelings.)*

Did the person listen to _____ when _____? *(Name another character and describe another event.)*

How do you feel when no one listens to you?

How do you think I feel when no one listens to me?

(Show a picture in the storybook.) This IS a _____. (He/she) IS wearing a _____ AND a _____ but NOT a _____.

HINT

Stress ICPS word concepts wherever possible—for instance, OR, AND, NOT, SAME-DIFFERENT.

Recognizing Happy, Sad, and Angry Feelings

LISTENING/NOT LISTENING

If you ALL talk at the SAME time, can I hear you with my ears?

When you do NOT listen to me, how do you think I feel?

How can you tell?

(Look sad.) You can see me with your _____. *(Point to eyes.)*

(Sound sad.) You can hear me with your _____. *(Point to ears.)*

TRANSITIONS

(To a child keeping the group waiting) How might the others feel if they have to wait and wait for you? *(If needed:* HAPPY or ANGRY?*)*

(On a very snowy day) If you do NOT put on your boots and you catch a cold, how will you feel? *(If the child says sick, add:* Sick and HAPPY or SAD?*)*

(At cleanup time) If you do NOT help clean up, how do you think I will feel? What can you do so I will NOT feel that way?

If the child knows the concepts and responds, "Happy," just say, "I know you're teasing me. How do you think I really feel?"

MINI-DIALOGUES

In these mini-dialogues, the teacher helps children identify their own feelings and prompts them to look and listen to find out about others' feelings.

Situation 1: Alan is unhappy and approaches the teacher.

Alan:	See my new shoes.
Teacher:	How do they make you feel?
Alan:	Mad.
Teacher:	Why do they make you feel mad?
Alan:	Because they hurt.

When Alan remarked on his new shoes, the teacher might have responded, "They're very nice," thus ending the conversation. The ICPS approach allowed this child to know that someone cared how he felt. It also helped the teacher understand that the child did comprehend the concept of anger and, contrary to expectation, the shoes did not please him.

Situation 2: Bev is unhappy and crying in a corner.

Teacher: *(To the group)* How does Bev feel? How can you tell? You can see her with your _____. *(Points dramatically to eyes.)* And you can hear her with your _____. *(Points dramatically to ears.)*

Notice how the teacher in the next two examples stresses ICPS words while using questions about how the children feel.

Situation 3: Steven is happy.

Teacher: *(To the group)* Who IS feeling HAPPY? Who is NOT feeling SAD? Do Steven AND _____ feel the SAME way OR a DIFFERENT way? How can you tell? You can see with your _____. *(Points dramatically to eyes.)* And you can hear with your _____. *(Points dramatically to ears.)*

Situation 4: Ben grabs a toy truck from Celia.

Teacher: *(To Ben)* What happened? What's the matter?

Ben: She's had it already.

Teacher: *(To Celia)* What do you think happened?

Celia: I'm not done making my road!

Teacher: *(To both)* It looks as though you two see what happened a DIFFERENT way. That means you have a problem. *(To Celia)* How did you feel when Ben grabbed the truck?

Celia: Mad.

Teacher: *(To Ben)* How did you feel about grabbing that?

Ben: I want it.

Teacher: *(To both)* Can either of you think of a way to solve this problem? A way so you'll both feel better? *(Or: What can you two do when you want to play with the SAME truck at the SAME time?)*

If response is reasonable: Go ahead and try that.

If response is successful: How do you feel now?

Finding Out How People Feel: Happy, Sad, Angry

LANGUAGE ARTS: STORY COMPREHENSION

Read any story. Reread and, at appropriate points, ask the following questions:

How did _____ feel when _____? *(Name a character in the story and describe an event—for example, he or she lost her favorite doll.)*

How could another person in the story help make _____ feel HAPPY again?

Do _____ and the other person feel the SAME way OR a DIFFERENT way about what happened in the story?

MATH

Who would feel HAPPIER with one *(show one finger)* than with two *(show two fingers)* pieces of candy?

(To a child who raises hand) Do you like candy? *(If the child answers yes, repeat the question.)*

Who would NOT be HAPPIER with two pieces of candy?

Do we ALL like the SAME thing?

If no: No, SOME of us like DIFFERENT things.

If yes: Yes, we ALL like candy.

SOCIAL STUDIES

Home and Family

What makes your mom HAPPY? SAD? ANGRY?

What do you do that makes your mom HAPPY? ANGRY?

Think of someone DIFFERENT who lives with you at home. *(If child gives a name:* Is that your sister OR your _____?)

What makes (him/her) feel HAPPY? SAD? ANGRY?

What do you do that makes (him/her) feel HAPPY? ANGRY?

Community

A police officer helped a lady cross the street. How do you think the lady felt?

A nurse at school checks your eyes and ears. How does that make you feel?

Does anyone feel a DIFFERENT way?

SCIENCE

If you have a dog at home, raise your hand.

How can you tell if your dog is HAPPY?

How can you tell if your dog is SAD? ANGRY?

Who has a DIFFERENT pet at home?

How can you tell if your _____ is HAPPY? SAD? ANGRY?

Does the sun come out in the day OR at night?

How do you feel when the sun comes out?

How do you feel when the sun does NOT come out (when it rains)?

Remembering Choices

PURPOSE

To stress the need to listen and pay attention and to give children practice in these skills

MATERIALS

For Option 1: Illustrations 5–7 (from Lesson 15)

TEACHER SCRIPT

Option 1

> **NOTE**
>
> Before beginning, duplicate and cut the animal pictures apart. Mount individually on thin posterboard.

Hold up pictures of the dog, bird, and rabbit.

(Child 1), come up to the front and choose one of these pictures—the dog, the bird, OR the rabbit.

Hold the picture to your chest, with the blank side facing out.

Don't show the other children your picture.

(Child 2), come up to the front.

(If Child 1 chooses the dog) Here we have the pictures of the bird and the rabbit.

Choose one of these and hold it up with the blank side facing the group.

Good. Now place the third picture face down.

(If Child 2 chooses the bird) (Child 3), who has the dog?

(Child 4), who has the rabbit?

Oh, no one does. I tried to trick you.

(Child 5), what picture does (Child 2) have?

If the children's ability allows, repeat the activity, but this time have three children make selections. You may wish to move children around at the front of the group so the same picture isn't always in the same position.

Option 2

(Child 1), what do you like to do at school? (*If needed:* If you could choose one, would you choose to paint OR play with blocks?)

(Child 2), what would you choose?

If (Child 2) repeats what (Child 1) says, ask the group, "Did Child 1 and Child 2 choose the SAME thing OR something DIFFERENT?" Then ask, "(Child 2), can you tell us something DIFFERENT you would choose?" Offer alternatives if necessary.

(Child 3), what did (Child 1) choose?

(Child 4), who chose the _____? (*Name something not chosen.*)
Oh, I tried to trick you. Very good.

(Child 5), what did (Child 2) choose?

(Child 6), is there something you do NOT like to do?

(Child 7), is there something you do NOT like to do?

(To the group) What did (Child 6) say (he/she) does NOT like to do?

What did (Child 7) say (he/she) does NOT like to do?

(Child 6), what do you like to do?

(Child 7), what do you like to do?

(To the group) What did (Child 6) say (he/she) does like to do?

What did (Child 6) say (he/she) does NOT like to do?

What did (Child 7) say (he/she) does like to do?

What did (Child 7) say (he/she) does NOT like to do?

Who remembers what (Child 1) chose?

Continue to ask about other children's choices as time and interest permit.

HINT

Prompt children as needed by naming choices—for example, "Who chose the sandbox?"

Listening and Paying Attention

Try helping children develop their listening and attention skills in the following curriculum areas.

LANGUAGE ARTS: VISUAL DISCRIMINATION

What's Missing?

Activity 1

Place three colored beads (marbles, balls, crayons) in a row.

Look carefully at these colors.

What color is this one? *(Point to red.)*

And this? *(Point to blue.)*

And this? *(Point to yellow.)*

Now close your eyes tight. No peeking!

Put your hands over your eyes so you can't see.

(Take away one of the objects.) Which one is NOT here?

Activity 2

Show the children five circles.

(Take away two of the circles.) Which ones are NOT here? The _____ one AND the _____ one.

Challenge the group according to ability by removing additional circles. Change the position of remaining circles so children have to remember colors, not just location.

LANGUAGE ARTS: AUDITORY DISCRIMINATION

Where's the Other One?

In advance, prepare six metal cans with lids by placing objects in them. Use three items of one type and three items of another type so that there will be duplicates. Objects should make different sounds when shaken in the can (for instance, pencils, beads, sand). The idea of this game is to find the cans that make the same sound.

> (Child 1), choose a can and shake it.
>
> All of you, listen to the sound and remember where that sound is.
>
> Now shake another can. Is that the SAME OR a DIFFERENT sound?
>
> (Child 2), now you pick a can and shake it.
>
> *If a different sound:* Shake another can and listen to the sound.
>
> *If the same sound as before:* Try to find the can that has the SAME sound.

Continue until all three sounds are matched. Expand the number of cans, if desired.

SCIENCE: CLASSIFICATION

> What do a dog AND a cat have?
>
> *If needed:* What do they have that you do NOT have?
>
> *If still needed:* How many legs?
>
> What else do a dog AND a cat have that you do NOT have?
>
> How are an apple AND a strawberry the SAME? (*If needed:* They are both red, both fruits.)
>
> How are they DIFFERENT?
>
> How are an apple AND an orange the SAME?
>
> How are they DIFFERENT?

Continue with other pairings as long as time and interest permit.

A Story

PURPOSE

To encourage story comprehension and further understanding of feelings, as well as sensitivity to the idea that not listening can affect someone's feelings

MATERIALS

Any storybook

TEACHER SCRIPT

Read any story to the class, then reread and, at appropriate points, ask the following questions:

How did _____ feel when _____? *(Name a character in the story and describe a specific event.)*

Why do you think (he/she) felt that way?

Would you feel the SAME way or a DIFFERENT way as _____ about that?

Use ICPS word concepts whenever possible—for example, "Did the person in the story _____ AND _____ OR _____ AND _____ ?")

Sample Story

Read Alexander and the Terrible, Horrible, No Good, Very Bad Day, *by Judith Viorst (Scholastic, Inc., 1972), then at the following specified points, ask these questions:*

After: ". . . all I found was breakfast cereal."

How did Alexander feel about that?

After: ". . . after school my mom took us all to the dentist and Dr. Fields found a cavity . . ."

How did Alexander feel about that?

After: "I am having a terrible, horrible, no good, very bad day, I told everybody."

Was anybody listening?

How did that make Alexander feel?

After: ". . . and I had to wear my railroad-train pajamas."

How did Alexander feel about that?

Discuss the following general questions:

Who can remember what happened that made Alexander feel he was having a terrible, horrible, no good, very bad day?

Would finding only breakfast cereal make you feel the SAME way as Alexander or a DIFFERENT way? (*If different:* Tell us why that would make you feel DIFFERENT.)

Would going to the dentist make you feel the SAME way as Alexander or a DIFFERENT way? (*If different:* Tell us why that would make you feel DIFFERENT.)

What else? Tell me new, DIFFERENT things that would make you feel you would be having a terrible, horrible, no good, very bad day.

Continue discussion as time and interest permit.

Why-Because, Might-Maybe

PURPOSE

To help children become aware that behavior has causes (WHY-BECAUSE) and to avoid quick and faulty assumptions about others (MIGHT-MAYBE)

MATERIALS

Any hand puppet (for example, Kookie the Crow)

TEACHER SCRIPT

Kookie: I'm Kookie the Crow. I came to play a game with you today. I came to play the WHY-BECAUSE Game. Let me show you how to play. First I'll play with your teacher. *(To teacher)* _____, I'm very tired.

Teacher: WHY?

Kookie: BECAUSE I forgot to take my nap.

Kookie: *(To the group)* Now I'm going to play with you. When I say something, you all ask real loud, WHY? Let's try it: I'm very hungry. Now you ask WHY.

Children: WHY?

Kookie: Very good. Now remember, ask WHY every time I say something. *(Pauses.)* I'm very hungry.

Children: WHY?

Kookie: BECAUSE I haven't had my lunch. *(Pauses.)* I like going to school.

Children: WHY?

Kookie: BECAUSE the children are my friends. *(Pauses.)* I can't sing today.

Children: WHY?

Kookie: BECAUSE my throat hurts. Now let's change the game. I'm going to ask you WHY, and you make up the BECAUSE. Now listen. *(To teacher)* I am going to the store. I am going to walk. I am NOT going to take the bus. Can you guess WHY I'm going to walk?

Teacher: BECAUSE it's a nice day out.

Kookie: MAYBE. Can you think of a DIFFERENT BECAUSE?

Teacher:	BECAUSE your friend is walking to the store and you want to walk with your friend.
Kookie:	*(To the group)* See, there is more than one BECAUSE. Now let's play together. *(Pauses.)* Johnny won't come to my house and play with me today. WHY won't Johnny come to my house and play with me today? Does anybody have a BECAUSE?
Children:	*(Respond.)*
Kookie:	MAYBE he won't come BECAUSE *(repeat response)*. Does anybody have a DIFFERENT BECAUSE? *(Go on until children run out of answers.)* Let's play this game again. *(Pauses.)* I like birthday parties. Can you guess WHY I like birthday parties?
Children:	*(Respond.)*
Kookie:	Very good. I MIGHT like birthday parties BECAUSE *(repeat response)*. Now let's think of a DIFFERENT BECAUSE. I like birthday parties BECAUSE _____.
Children:	*(Respond.)*
Teacher:	Very good. Why does Kookie like birthday parties? MAYBE it's BECAUSE *(repeat first answer)* OR BECAUSE *(repeat second answer)* OR BECAUSE *(repeat next answer, and so forth)*.
Kookie:	Why is _____ NOT here today? *(Name an absent child and let the group respond.)* MAYBE. Who can think of a DIFFERENT BECAUSE?

HINT

An extremely verbal child may give long, drawn-out responses, consistently be the first to respond, and in general dominate the group without meaning to. To avoid losing the interest of such a child, try saying, "You just had a long turn. Now a DIFFERENT child needs a turn." The dominating child can then be encouraged to "pick someone who has NOT had a turn." Using ICPS word concepts in this way prevents such a child from feeling frustrated, withdrawing, or becoming disruptive.

Feelings Have Causes

PURPOSE

To illustrate that feelings have causes and to lay the foundation for the idea that children can influence others' feelings through their own actions

MATERIALS

Illustration 9

TEACHER SCRIPT

Show children Illustration 9.

How does this boy *(point to boy with ball)* feel? *(If needed:* Does he feel HAPPY or SAD?)

MAYBE he feels HAPPY. Why do you think he MIGHT be HAPPY?

BECAUSE _____.

This boy MIGHT be HAPPY BECAUSE *(repeat response).* That's one BECAUSE.

The idea of this game is to think of lots of reasons, lots of DIFFERENT BECAUSES.

Why else MIGHT this boy be HAPPY?

He MIGHT be HAPPY BECAUSE *(repeat first reason)* OR BECAUSE *(repeat second reason)* OR BECAUSE *(repeat third reason, and so forth).*

(Point to boy receiving ball.) How MIGHT this boy feel? *(Repeat previous line of questioning.)*

HINT

It is important when the first child responds that you say, "That's *one* BECAUSE" or "That MIGHT be WHY. Now the idea of the game is to think of lots of DIFFERENT BECAUSES." In this way, the first child understands that you are asking for more answers because that is the purpose of the game and not because you think the answer was incorrect.

It is also important to ask a child to explain an unexpected response. One child answered that the receiver in the illustration felt sad. When his teacher asked him why, the child replied that the boy in the picture was afraid he would get hit in the eye. Had the teacher not asked why, she might have assumed the child did not yet understand the concept when, in fact, the child had something equally relevant on his mind.

ILLUSTRATION 9 Lesson 24

More Than One Because

PURPOSE

To review the relationship between causes and feelings

MATERIALS

Illustration 10

TEACHER SCRIPT

Today's ICPS game is about the SAME words we learned in our last two games. Does anyone remember what those words are?

Yes, the words WHY-BECAUSE and MIGHT-MAYBE.

Show children Illustration 10.

Look at this picture. How is this girl *(point)* feeling?

How can you tell? (*If crying is given as an answer:* How can you tell she is crying?)

You can see with your _____.

WHY is this girl SAD?

WHY MIGHT she be falling on her skates? *(Let children respond.)*

That's *one* BECAUSE. Let's think of lots of DIFFERENT BECAUSES.

Elicit several possible reasons. If needed, direct attention to the tree or the crack in the sidewalk: Maybe she bumped into the tree or fell over the crack.

What can this boy *(point)* do OR say to make this girl feel HAPPY? *(Let children respond.)*

That's *one* way. Can anyone think of a DIFFERENT way to help her feel HAPPY?

Repeat as long as time and interest permit.

HINT

Emphasize the word *one* when you say, "That's *one* way" here and in following lessons to suggest the existence of other possible alternatives.

ILLUSTRATION 10 Lesson 25

What Do You Choose?
A Different Because

PURPOSE

To show children that DIFFERENT people have DIFFERENT BECAUSES
for their choices

MATERIALS

Illustrations 11 and 12

TEACHER SCRIPT

Show children Illustration 11.

Where are these children playing?

Good, in the park.

Show children Illustration 12.

Where is this child *(point)?*

Yes, sick in bed. Why MIGHT she be sick in bed? *(Let children
respond.)*

Just like the game before, when you chose one animal, you can
choose one place to be—playing in the park OR sick in bed.

But this time, I want you to tell me WHY.

(Child 1), which place would you choose?

*If the child does not respond verbally, help the child point to the one he or she
would choose.*

(Child 2), which one would you choose? Only one.

(Child 1) chose the _____ AND (Child 2) chose the _____.

Did (Child 1) AND (Child 2) choose the SAME thing OR something
DIFFERENT?

Yes, they chose (the SAME/a DIFFERENT) thing.

Repeat with several pairs.

> *(To a child who chose the park)* WHY did you choose the park?
>
> BECAUSE _____.

Repeat with others who chose the park. Ask each child for a different BECAUSE.

> *(To a child who chose being sick in bed)* WHY did you choose being sick in bed?
>
> BECAUSE _____.

Repeat with others who chose being sick in bed. Ask each child for a different BECAUSE.

> Is it OK that *(name a child who chose the park)* chose something DIFFERENT from *(name a child who chose being sick in bed)*?
>
> Yes, it is OK for DIFFERENT children to choose DIFFERENT things.
>
> Did ALL of you choose the SAME thing?
>
> No, ALL of you did NOT choose the SAME thing.
>
> SOME of you chose things that are _____. *(If needed:* The SAME or DIFFERENT?)

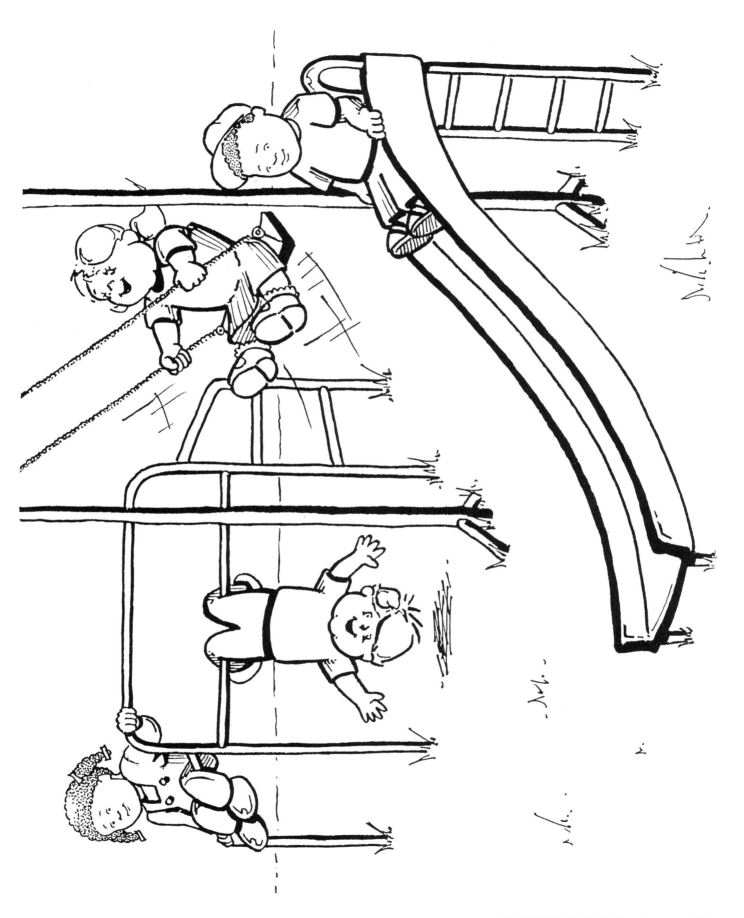

ILLUSTRATION 11 Lesson 26

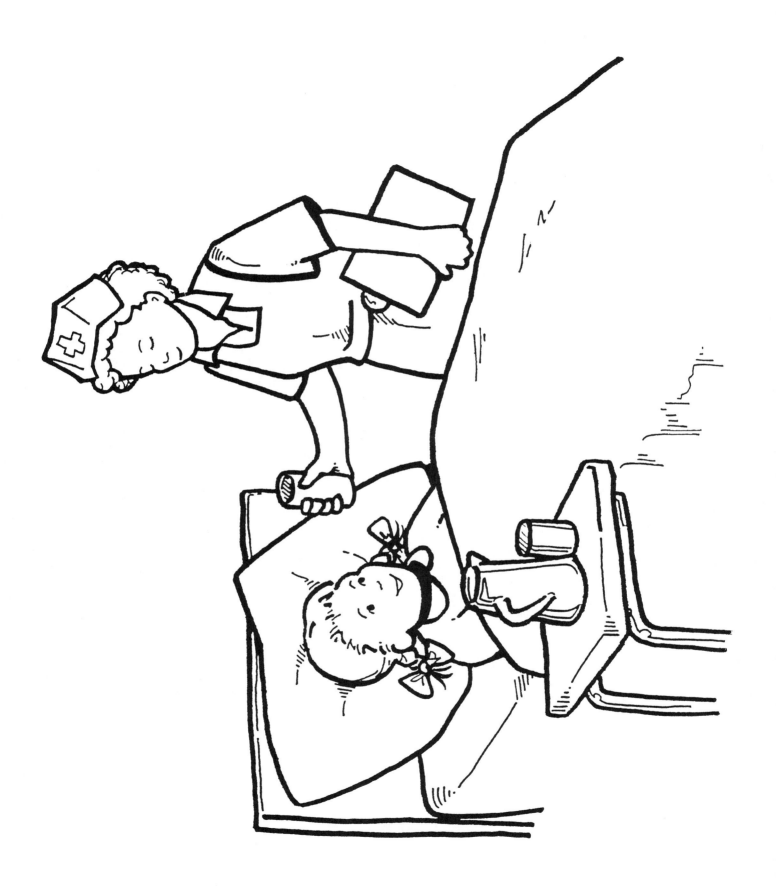

ILLUSTRATION 12   Lesson 26

Feelings and Causes,
ICPS Words: Might-Maybe

Good problem solvers think about their own and others' feelings.
Your child is learning that people can feel DIFFERENT ways about the
SAME thing. Try asking your child about feelings and their causes.

WHEN WATCHING TV OR READING A STORY

Do you think _____ is feeling HAPPY OR SAD about what
happened? *(Let the child respond.)*

(He/she) MIGHT feel that way.

Would you feel the SAME way or a DIFFERENT way about that?

IN THE GROCERY STORE

When you nag (bother) me like that for candy, how do you think I feel?

What can you do so I will NOT feel that way?

I MIGHT NOT feel that way. What else can you do? *(Let the child respond.)*

Good thinking. You thought of two things you can do.

WHEN YOU ARE ANGRY OR SAD

Try saying this when your child is not the cause of your anger or sadness:

I feel (ANGRY/SAD) now. Can you tell me WHY? *(Let the child respond.)*

MAYBE it's BECAUSE _____. *(Repeat the child's reason.)*

Can you think of something DIFFERENT to do until I feel better?

Try saying this when your child is the cause of your anger or sadness:

I feel (ANGRY/SAD) now. Can you tell me WHY? *(Let the child respond.)*

MAYBE it's BECAUSE _____. *(Repeat the child's reason.)*

How do you think I feel when you (don't listen, throw your food, and so on)?

What can you do so I will NOT feel this way?

YOUR IDEAS

_____

_____

_____

_____

_____

A Story

PURPOSE

To review WHY-BECAUSE and help children see things from different perspectives

MATERIALS

Any storybook

TEACHER SCRIPT

Read any storybook to the class, then reread and, at appropriate points, ask the following questions:

Who can remember what _____ did when _____?
(Name a character in the story and describe a specific event.)

WHY do you think the person did that?

Can you think of a DIFFERENT BECAUSE?

How do you think _____ felt when _____?
(Name another character in the story and repeat the event.)

Did _____ AND _____ feel the SAME way about that?

If no: No, they felt a _____ way.

If needed: SAME OR DIFFERENT?

How would that make you feel?

Would you feel the SAME way the person did OR a DIFFERENT way?

Tell us WHY you would feel that way.

Review

PURPOSE

To strengthen understanding of ICPS concepts presented thus far

MATERIALS

Illustration 3 (from Lesson 11), Illustration 4 (from Lesson 12), Illustration 8 (from Lesson 17), and Illustration 13 (from this lesson)

TEACHER SCRIPT

Call on different children, or let them raise their hands to answer the following questions:

Tell me who has on a shirt that IS (for example, red).

Who has on a shirt that is NOT (red)?

(Child 1) has on a blouse that IS (blue).

Who has on a blouse that IS the SAME color?

Who has on a blouse that IS a DIFFERENT color?

(Child 1) may jump.

(Child 2) may NOT jump.

May (Child 1) jump?

Yes, go ahead and jump.

May (Child 2) jump?

No, (Child 2) may NOT jump.

(Child 2), do something DIFFERENT.

(Child 3), do the SAME thing that (Child 2) just did.

(Child 4), pat your head AND stamp your foot.

Now pat your head, but do NOT stamp your foot.

Show children Illustrations 3, 4, 8, and 13. Four children can come up to the front and each hold one picture for the group to see. Ask the group the following questions:

Show me someone who IS SAD.

Show me someone who is NOT SAD.

Show me someone DIFFERENT who is NOT SAD.

Show me someone who IS HAPPY.

Show me someone who feels a DIFFERENT way.

Who else feels a DIFFERENT way?

WHY MIGHT this child *(point to Illustration 3)* feel HAPPY?
BECAUSE _____.
Who can tell me a DIFFERENT BECAUSE?

WHY MIGHT this child *(point to Illustration 4)* feel SAD?
BECAUSE _____.
Who can tell me a DIFFERENT BECAUSE?

How does this child *(point to Illustration 8)* feel?

How can you tell?

Can you hear him with your ears?

Can you ask this child in the picture?

What can you do? *(If needed:* You can see him with your _____.)

Name a boy in this room. Name SOME boys.

Name a girl who is wearing the color (green).

Name ALL the girls wearing the color (green).

ILLUSTRATION 13   Lesson 28

Do You Like?

PURPOSE

To suggest that asking, "Do you like" is another way of recognizing individual differences

MATERIALS

Illustrations 14–16

TEACHER SCRIPT

Show children Illustration 14.

Who can tell me what this *(point to apple)* is?

Yes, an apple.

Who can tell me what this *(point to carrot)* is?

Yes, a carrot.

(Child 1), if you could choose one and only one of these, which one would you choose?

(Child 2), would you choose the SAME thing OR would you choose something DIFFERENT?

Show children Illustration 15.

Who can tell me what this *(point to banana)* is?

Yes, a banana.

Who can tell me what this *(point to grapes)* is?

Yes, some grapes.

Who would NOT choose some grapes?

Who would choose some grapes?

Did _____ AND _____ choose the SAME thing OR something DIFFERENT?

Show children Illustration 16.

Who knows what this *(point to corn)* is?

Good, an ear of corn.

And this? *(Point to strawberry.)*

Yes, a strawberry.

Show children all three illustrations at once. Let three children come up to the front and each hold one for the group to see.

A new way to find out what people like is to ask, "Do you like?"

(Child 3), do you like strawberries?

Do you like carrots?

(Child 4), do you like grapes?

Do you like apples?

(Child 5), would you choose the strawberry *(point)* OR the carrot *(point)?*

Which one do you think (Child 6) would choose?

How can you find out? *(If needed:* Go ahead and ask, "Do you like?")

What's our new way of asking?

Yes, ask, "Do you like?"

(Child 7), would you choose the apple OR the banana?

Which one do you think (Child 8) would choose?

How can you find out? *(If needed:* Go ahead and ask.)

(Child 9), do you like horses?

Do you like swings?

Do you like to paint?

If yes to all three: (Child 9) likes horses AND swings AND painting.

If no to one or more: (Child 9) does like (horses) AND (painting). (He/she) does NOT like (swings).

HINT

Let children take the role of leader, asking, "Do you like?" about the illustrations or anything else they choose. Let them get carried away with the phrase.

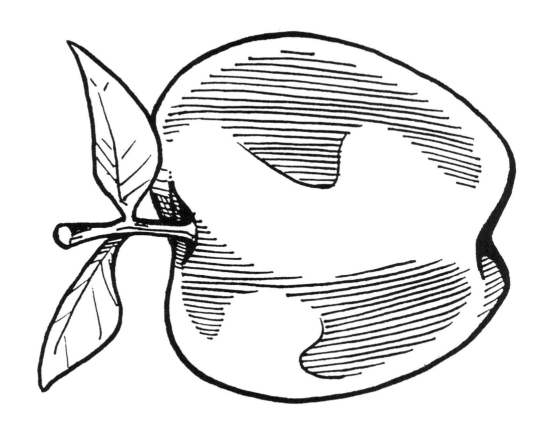

ILLUSTRATION 14   Lesson 29

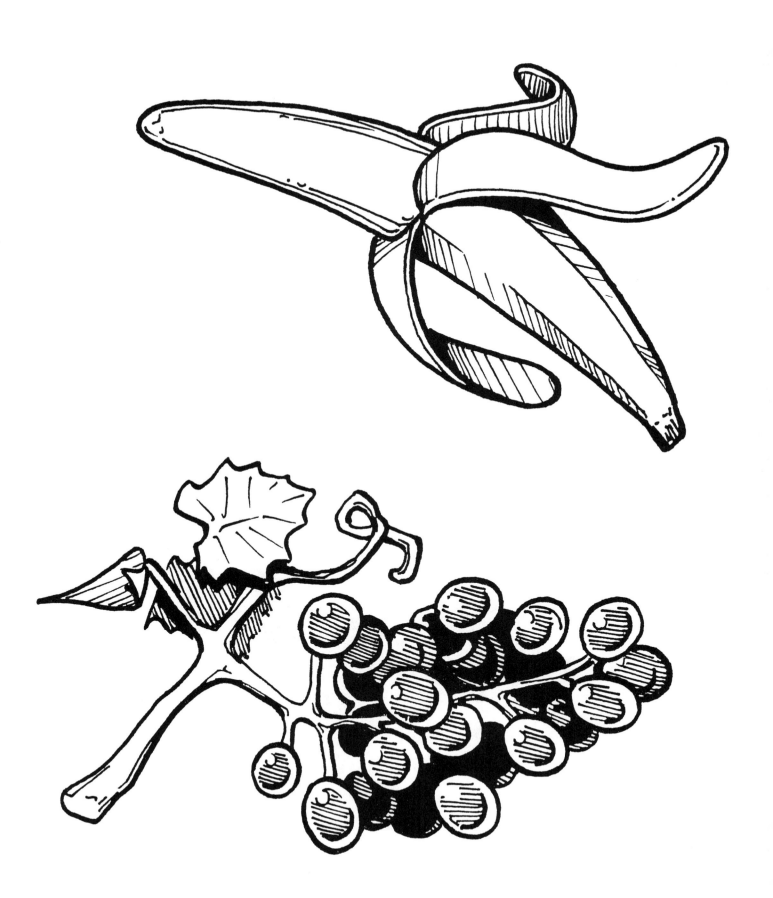

ILLUSTRATION 15   Lesson 29

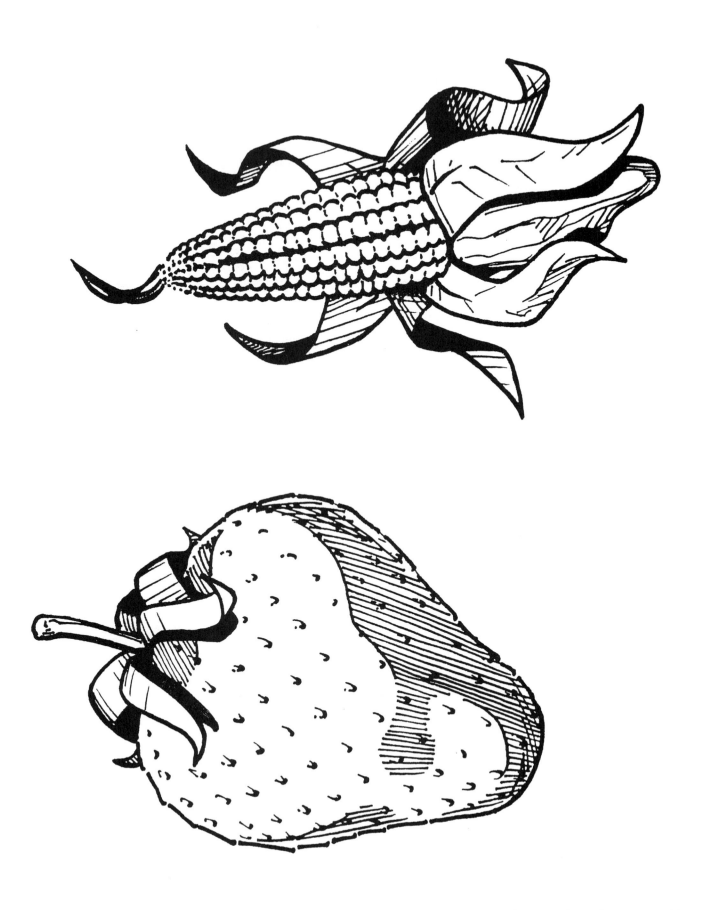

ILLUSTRATION 16   Lesson 29

Allie the Alligator, Part I

PURPOSE

To help children understand that feelings can change

MATERIALS

Two hand puppets (for example, Allie the Alligator and Whipple the Whale)

TEACHER SCRIPT

Allie: I am Allie the Alligator. I can NOT run and play with the children. My legs are too little. I wish I could run and play with the children.

Teacher: *(With a sad voice, turning the puppet's head down)* How does Allie the Alligator feel? *(Let children respond.)* Why does she feel SAD? BECAUSE _____. Well, one day a big whale, Whipple the Whale, saw Allie crying. *(Bring whale out on other hand.)*

Whipple: Allie, WHY are you so SAD?

Allie: BECAUSE I can NOT run and play with my friends.

Whipple: But you can swim. You can swim faster than all the other alligators. All the other alligators want you to play with them. They like you very much.

Teacher: Allie smiled and laughed. *(Open Allie's mouth wide.)*

Allie: *(With mouth wide open)* How do I feel now? *(Let children respond.)* Yes, HAPPY. *(With head down, pull mouth in)* How did I feel when I only thought about NOT being able to run with my friends? *(Let children respond.)* Yes, SAD. *(Mouth open wide)* Now I am HAPPY. *(Mouth in, head down)* Before, I was SAD. See, I can feel DIFFERENT ways at DIFFERENT times.

Teacher: Guess what? While Allie and Whipple were swimming *(mimic swimming motions)*, Allie found out she could do new tricks. She could somersault, and she could twist and turn. *(Demonstrate both.)*

Ask children what they remember about the story. The following questions may be helpful:

(Show one puppet.) What is this puppet's name?

(Show the other puppet.) And this puppet?

WHY did Allie feel SAD?

What made her feel HAPPY?

What could she do faster than all the other alligators?

What tricks could she do in the water?

Can you think of any other tricks you can teach her?

Let several children answer, then come up and teach Allie a new trick.

HINT

If a shy nonresponder imitates another child, remember not to push. Simply say, "Good, you showed us, too."

Allie the Alligator, Part II

PURPOSE

To help children learn to avoid faulty conclusions about someone else's preferences by asking, "Do you like?"

MATERIALS

The same hand puppets used in Lesson 30 (for example, Allie the Alligator and Whipple the Whale)

TEACHER SCRIPT

Teacher: Here's Allie the Alligator again. Before, we found out that Allie loves to swim. How did she feel when she was swimming before? (*If needed:* Did she feel HAPPY or SAD?) Yes, she felt very HAPPY BECAUSE she loves to swim. She's a very fast swimmer, too.

Allie: I've been swimming all morning. This morning some of my friends asked me to swim with them, and I said yes. They know I love to swim. (*Bring Whipple the Whale in slowly from the side.*) Here comes one of my friends, Whipple the Whale. He loves to swim, too.

Whipple: Hi, Allie. We sure had fun swimming this morning. We both love to swim, don't we? Let's go swimming now again. That would make me very HAPPY.

Allie: (*Pulls mouth in and holds head down so she looks sad.*)

Whipple: What's the matter, Allie? WHY do you look so SAD? I thought it would make you HAPPY if I asked you to swim.

Allie: I was HAPPY when we swam this morning. We swam for a long time. I would NOT be HAPPY to swim again this afternoon.

Whipple: (*To the group*) I guess she doesn't want to play with me this afternoon. Gee, I wish she'd play with me. I'll have to think of something so she'll want to play with me. Oh, I know what I'll do. (*Enthusiastically, to Allie*) Allie, if you don't want to swim right now, do you want to play with my new ball?

Allie: No! I don't like that game.

Whipple:	*(Puts head down, then enthusiastically, to Allie)* Would you like to go find some food to eat?
Allie:	Not now. I just ate, and I'm NOT hungry.
Whipple:	Gee, Allie, I really want to do something with you. What would you like to do now?
Allie:	I'd like to play hide-and-seek.
Whipple:	OK. I'd like that, too. I'm glad I asked you. I thought MAYBE you didn't want to play with me this afternoon.
Allie:	Oh, no. I like you. I just didn't want to swim because I wanted to do something DIFFERENT now. MAYBE tomorrow we can swim again. MAYBE tomorrow I will want to swim again.
Whipple:	OK. Let's play hide-and-seek now.
Teacher:	*(Hide Allie behind your back and have Whipple find her.)* Allie and Whipple played hide-and-seek for a while and were very HAPPY. The next day they went swimming again.
Allie:	*(To the group)* Do I like to swim ALL the time? *(Let children respond.)* No, sometimes I like to swim, and sometimes I do NOT like to swim. If I swim too much, I MIGHT get tired.
	(To Child 1) Do you like to run? (*If no:* What do you like to do?)
	(To the same child) Do you like to run ALL of the time or SOME of the time? I bet you would feel tired if you ran ALL of the time.

Ask children what they remember about the story. The following questions may be helpful:

Does Allie like to swim ALL of the time or SOME of the time?

WHY didn't Allie want to swim this afternoon?

Did Allie want to play with Whipple's new ball?

Why NOT? BECAUSE _____.

Did Allie want to go find food to eat?

Why NOT? BECAUSE _____.

What did Allie want to do?

How did Whipple find that out? (*If needed:* Did he ask her OR did he scream at her?)

When Whipple asked Allie to swim and Allie didn't want to, Whipple thought something that was NOT true. Was it that Allie was a bird, that Allie was sick, OR that Allie did NOT want to play with him?

Let children hold Allie or Whipple and ask others, "Do you like?" Then follow up with "Do you like to (repeat child's answer) ALL of the time or SOME of the time?" You may leave these puppets as "characters" in the classroom. Children may use them to create their own stories.

HINT

An effective technique for the shy nonresponder is to let the child hold the puppet and *be* Allie or Whipple. Ask, "Allie, what do you like to do?" If necessary, you can ask, "Do you like to swim?" The child can be encouraged to shake the puppet's head yes or no. You can follow with, "Do you like to play with blocks?" The extreme nonresponder can hold the puppet and be encouraged to open and close the puppet's mouth while you read a story. Often such children will begin to talk as the puppet and then, slowly, as themselves.

Using the Allie the Alligator Story

MINI-DIALOGUES

The following examples show how the teacher can help children apply their understanding of SOME-ALL concepts to avoid frustration.

Situation 1: Amy wants to ride the bike during storytime.

Teacher: Do you remember what Allie the Alligator likes to do?

Amy: Swim.

Teacher: Does Allie like to swim ALL of the time or SOME of the time?

Amy: SOME of the time.

Teacher: Do you like to ride the bike ALL of the time or SOME of the time?

If the child says "All of the time," say, casually, "I know you're teasing me." The next example illustrates this approach.

Situation 2: Eric wants to go outside during indoor free play.

Teacher: Do you like to be outside ALL of the time or SOME of the time?

Eric: ALL of the time.

Teacher: Oh, you're just teasing me. Can you think of something to do inside?

Eric: *(Angrily)* No!

Teacher: I know if you think real hard, you can think of something to do.

Eric: I'll play with Sandra.

Teacher: Good thinking. You thought of that all by yourself.

Situation 3: Shelly is feeling rejected because her friend JoAnn doesn't want to play with her.

Shelly: No one will play with me.

Teacher: Do you know WHY?

Shelly: No.

Teacher: Who do you want to play with?

Shelly: JoAnn.

Teacher: Did JoAnn play with you today?

Shelly: Yeah. We played hospital.

Teacher: Do you like to play with JoAnn ALL of the time or SOME of the time?

Shelly: SOME of the time.

Teacher: Do you think JoAnn likes to play with you ALL of the time or SOME of the time?

Shelly: SOME of the time.

Teacher: What is JoAnn doing now?

Shelly: Playing with Karen and Tammy.

Teacher: Can you think of something DIFFERENT to do now so you will feel HAPPY?

This kind of dialoguing guides the child to take both points of view. If JoAnn hadn't played with Shelly already that day, the teacher might have said, "Can you think of something to do or say so Karen and Tammy will let you play with them?"

Situation 4: Gregory wants Elizabeth to play, but Elizabeth says no.

Gregory: Elizabeth, let's play Lotto.

Elizabeth: No, I don't want to.

Gregory: *(Very sadly)* Please.

Elizabeth: *(Continues to shake her head no.)*

Teacher: Gregory, do you want to play with Elizabeth OR do you want to play Lotto?

Gregory: I want to play with Elizabeth.

Teacher: You and Elizabeth already played Lotto, right?

Gregory: Right.

Teacher: Do you think Elizabeth likes to play Lotto ALL of the time or SOME of the time?

Gregory: SOME of the time.

Teacher: How can you find out what Elizabeth likes to do?

Gregory: Ask her.

Teacher: Go ahead and ask her.

Gregory: *(To Elizabeth)* Do you like to paint?

Elizabeth: No.

Gregory: Do you like to jump?

Elizabeth: No.

Gregory: Do you like puzzles?

Elizabeth: Yes.

Gregory: Will you do puzzles with me?

Elizabeth: Yes.

Notice how Gregory used the question "Do you like?" to find out what Elizabeth wanted to do. He didn't give up too soon.

Is That Fair?

PURPOSE

To help children understand equal benefits when situations are equal and understand the rights of others when decisions are made

MATERIALS

A penny (or other small item) for each child in the group

TEACHER SCRIPT

Today's ICPS game is about the word FAIR.

I have a penny here for each of you, and I'm going to let each of you take one.

I only have enough pennies for each of you to have one.

Is it FAIR for each child to have one penny? *(Let children respond.)*

Yes, it is FAIR for each child to have one penny BECAUSE I only have enough for each of you to have one.

If (Child 1) takes two pennies, then somebody will not have a penny. Is that FAIR?

No, it is NOT FAIR for one child to have two pennies and for someone else NOT to have any.

How would you feel if you wanted a penny and did NOT get one?

Yes, you would feel (SAD/ANGRY).

WHY would you feel (SAD/ANGRY)? BECAUSE _____.

It is NOT FAIR for one child to have two pennies and another child NOT to have any.

Can you think of something else a child MIGHT do that is NOT FAIR? *(Elicit different responses.)*

If two children want to look at a storybook and one keeps it and does NOT let the other one see it, is that FAIR?

No, that is NOT FAIR.

If two children want to look at a storybook, what is FAIR?

Is it FAIR to share the storybook and look at it together?

Yes, it is FAIR to share the storybook.

Is it FAIR to take turns with the storybook? To let one child look at it and when that child is finished, let the other child look at it?

Yes, it is FAIR to take turns with the storybook.

WHY is it FAIR to share or to take turns?

How would (Child 2) feel if (Child 3) did NOT let (him/her) see the storybook?

Yes, (he/she) would feel (SAD/ANGRY).

It is FAIR to take turns. That means for one child to look at the storybook and when finished to let the next child look at it.

It is also FAIR to look at the storybook together—to share it—if both children want to do that.

Is it FAIR for one child to look at a storybook and then keep it so that the next child can NOT see it?

WHY is that NOT FAIR?

What is FAIR?

More About Fair

PURPOSE

To illustrate that in being FAIR, it is sometimes necessary to wait

MATERIALS

Chairs or big blocks that can be used to build a pretend car

TEACHER SCRIPT

Today we're going to talk about what's FAIR again.

Let's go on a pretend trip to the zoo. We will go in a car.

Let's pretend the car is only big enough to take SOME of you. It is NOT big enough to take ALL of you.

SOME of you can go now, and SOME will go later.

Have children help you build a car out of chairs or big blocks.

Let's pretend that now *(name half of the children in the group)* will go on our pretend trip.

For now, *(name the rest of the group)* will have to stay here BECAUSE the car is NOT big enough for all of you.

All the children over here *(point to the first half)* are going on the trip. The rest of you will get to go later.

(To the rest) Wait for us here—we'll be back soon.

(To the whole group) If you're going on the trip now, raise your hand.

If any children incorrectly identify themselves, help them get into the proper group.

OK, if you're going on the trip now, let's open the door and get in.

Go through the motion of opening the door and helping children get seated.

Let's pretend we're riding. *(Demonstrate by bouncing.)*

Can we make the sound of a horn? Let's all ride.

Now we're at the zoo. I see a zebra. What do you see? *(Have children name animals they see.)*

Very good. Now we're back. We had a fun ride, didn't we?

Let's open the door and get out.

Go through the motion of opening the door and helping children get out.

Now I'm going on another trip with SOME children.

We're going in the SAME car, and I can only take SOME of you.

Who should go on the trip?

From raised hands, pick one child who did not go the first time and one who did go the first time.

Did (Child 1) go on the first trip? *(Name a child who did not go on the first trip.)*

Did (Child 2) go on the first trip? *(Name a child who did go.)*

Is it FAIR for (Child 1) to go now?

WHY is it FAIR for this child to go now?

Yes, it is FAIR BECAUSE (he/she) did NOT go on the first trip.

Is it FAIR for (Child 2) to go now? Remember, (he/she) did go on the first trip.

WHY is it NOT FAIR for (Child 2) to go now?

That's right, it is NOT FAIR for (Child 2) to go now BECAUSE (he/she) went the first time. We have to give everybody a chance to go.

Name each child in the group and ask whether it would be fair for that child to go on the second trip, and why. If necessary, ask children whether a particular child went on the first trip or not. Be sure to go on the pretend trip with the second group.

HINT

To a child who is dominating the group, you can say, for example, "Paula, is it FAIR for you to have ALL of the turns and for other children NOT to have any?" Then ask the child, "Who has NOT had a chance?"

Fair or Not Fair?

REFUSAL TO SHARE

Is it FAIR for you to have ALL the turns and for _____ NOT to have any?

How MIGHT _____ feel if you do NOT let (him/her) have a turn?

What can you do that is FAIR so _____ won't feel that way?

This line of questioning can also be useful when a child is refusing to share toys or classroom supplies.

DOMINATING BEHAVIORS

How do people feel when they want to say something and you keep shouting out?

Who has NOT had a chance to talk?

(To a child who is dominating the group) Can you pick someone who has NOT had a chance to talk?

PROBLEM-SOLVING SKILLS

ALTERNATIVE SOLUTIONS

The lessons in this section help children learn that there is more than one way to solve a problem. In particular, they stimulate children to think of as many different solutions as possible to everyday interpersonal problems and encourage a *process* of thinking: "There's more than one way"; "I don't have to give up so soon."

PROCEDURE

As used in the lessons, the general procedure for eliciting alternative solutions is as follows:

1. State the problem or have the child state the problem.

2. Say that the idea is to think of lots of DIFFERENT ways to solve this problem.

3. Write all of the children's ideas on chalkboard or easel. (Even though children may not be able to read, they like your writing what they say.)

4. Ask for the first solution. If the solution is relevant, repeat it and identify it as *one* way to solve the problem. Remind children that the object is to think of lots of DIFFERENT ways to solve the problem.

5. Ask for another solution, and so forth.

6. When ideas run out, probe for further solutions by saying, "What can _____ say to *(repeat problem)?*" and "What can _____ do to *(repeat problem)?*"

ENUMERATIONS

Children often give variations of the same solution. For example:

- *Giving something:* Give him candy, give him gum, give him a cookie.

- *Hurting someone:* Hit him, kick him, bite him.

- *Telling someone:* Tell his mother, father, sister.

An effective way of dealing with enumerations is to say, for example, "Giving candy and giving gum are kind of the SAME BECAUSE they are both giving something. Can you think of something DIFFERENT from giving something?'' After a while, you can ask children to identify for themselves how enumerations show the same kinds of ideas.

Avoid saying, ''That's good'' or ''That's a good idea'' in response to a given solution. If you focus on the *content* of what children say, they will think you like a particular idea and you will likely get more enumerations. If you do say *good,* focus on the *process* by saying, ''Good, that's a DIFFERENT idea.''

UNCLEAR OR
APPARENTLY IRRELEVANT RESPONSES

If a child gives an apparently irrelevant response, it is important to ask, ''WHY do you think that will solve this problem?'' or to say, ''Tell us a little more about that.'' Often a response that seems irrelevant is actually logical.

Take, for instance, the problem of a boy's wanting an extra piece of cake at school. The solution ''He'll say he'll get fat'' may appear to be a consequence of eating the cake (a concept to come later). You might be tempted to assume that the response is therefore irrelevant to the present lesson. However, if you ask, ''How would that help the boy get the cake?'' the child might say, ''Because he's too skinny, and his mom wants him to eat more.'' The new information shows that the response ''He'll say he'll get fat'' is indeed a solution—a way to help the boy get the extra cake. If on clarification a response actually does turn out to be a consequence instead of a solution, acknowledge the response and elicit a solution by asking, 'What can the boy do or say to solve the problem?''

''He will cry'' is another response requiring clarification. If in the case of the boy who wants the extra cake the response is simply a *reaction* to the problem's existence, it is irrelevant because it is not a solution to the problem. If, on the other hand, the response is intended to gain sympathy, it is a *cognitive cry*—and therefore a solution. If a child gives this response, always ask him or her to tell you more.

What's the Problem?

PURPOSE

To help children understand what a problem is and begin to think of alternative ways to solve it

MATERIALS

Illustration 17

Chalkboard or easel

TEACHER SCRIPT

Show children Illustration 17.

> Let's pretend these girls were playing with these toys *(point)* and it's time to put them away.
>
> There is a problem here. A problem is when something is wrong—something is the matter.
>
> Let's pretend this girl *(point to the girl walking away)* is going to leave and won't help this girl *(point to the other girl)* put the toys away.
>
> Now remember, both girls were playing with the toys.
>
> Was this girl *(point to the first girl)* playing?
>
> Was this girl *(point to the second girl)* playing?
>
> Who should help put the toys away?
>
> Is it FAIR for this girl *(point to the girl standing by toys)* to put ALL of the toys away and for this girl *(point to the girl walking away)* NOT to help?
>
> Is it FAIR for both girls to help clean up?
>
> WHY is it FAIR for both girls to help clean up? BECAUSE _____.
>
> Yes, it is FAIR for both girls to help clean up BECAUSE they were both playing.

So the problem is that this girl *(point to the girl walking away)* will NOT help clean up, put the toys away.

Now, what can this girl *(point to the girl standing by toys)* do or say so the other girl will help her put the toys away?

I'm going to write ALL your ideas on the chalkboard. Let's fill up the whole board.

Write each response as given to form a numbered list. Although the children cannot read their responses, writing them is a powerful motivating technique.

RESPONSE: She could ask her. *(Write this on the board, as the example shows.)*

1. She could ask her.

If the response is relevant: That's *one* way. Now the idea of this game is to think of lots of DIFFERENT ways to solve the problem.

If the response is not relevant: How would that help solve the problem?

OK, she could ask her. That's *one* way.

Now the idea of this game is to think of lots of DIFFERENT ways that this girl *(point to the girl standing by toys)* can get this girl *(point to the girl walking away)* to help her put the toys away.

Who's got way number two to solve this problem? *(Show two fingers.)* That means a way to make things better.

RESPONSE: She could give her candy. *(Add to the list.)*

1. She could ask her.
2. She could give her candy.

That's a DIFFERENT way. So now we have two ways.

She could ask her OR she could give her candy. Let's ALL say, together, "OR."

Who has way number three? *(Show three fingers.)*

RESPONSE: She could give her gum. *(Enumeration—write under the like response, not as a separate solution.)*

1. She could ask her.
2. She could give her candy.
   She could give her gum.

Giving her candy and giving her gum are kind of the SAME BECAUSE they are both giving her something.

Can you think of something DIFFERENT from giving her something?

RESPONSE: She could say she won't be her friend. *(Add to the list.)*

Yes. Way number one, she could ask her.

Way number two, she could give her candy or gum.

Way number three, she could say she won't be her friend.

1. She could ask her.
2. She could give her candy.
   She could give her gum.
3. She could say she won't be her friend.

What else can she do?

Let's ALL say together, "What else?"

Let's fill the whole board.

Continue to generate other solutions as time and interest permit. When finished, summarize the different ways, holding up the appropriate number of fingers for each one.

HINT

If desired, you can quicken the pace of this and other lessons in which you use the board by writing just key words—for example, "ask," "give candy," and so forth.

Remember to avoid saying a particular solution is good. You will just get enumerations. If you say "good," reinforce the *process*, not the *content*, of thinking. For instance, say, "Good, you gave another way" or "Good, you thought of a DIFFERENT idea."

ILLUSTRATION 17   Lesson 34

What Else Can He Do?

PURPOSE

To encourage children to think of alternative solutions to another problem

MATERIALS

Illustration 18
Chalkboard or easel

TEACHER SCRIPT

Show children Illustration 18.

> The problem in this picture is that this boy *(point)* wants his mother to buy him this sailboat.
>
> What does this boy want his mother to do? *(Let children respond.)*
>
> Now we're going to play the What Else Can He Do Game. We want to think of lots of ways, lots of DIFFERENT ways, to solve this problem.
>
> I'm going to write your ideas on the chalkboard. Who's got way number one? *(Show one finger.)*
>
> RESPONSE: He could ask her. *(Write this and other responses on the board, as shown in Lesson 34.)*
>
> *If the response is relevant:* That's *one* way. Now the idea of this game is to think of lots of DIFFERENT ways to solve the problem.
>
> *If the response is not relevant:* How will that help solve the problem?
>
> That's *one* way. That MIGHT solve the problem, make it better.
>
> Now the idea of this game is to think of lots of DIFFERENT ways that this boy can get his mom to buy him the sailboat.
>
> Who's got way number two? *(Show two fingers.)*
>
> RESPONSE: He could say he'll share it with his sister.
> *(Add to the list.)*

OK, way number one, he could ask her.

Way number two, he could say he'll share it with his sister.

Who's got a DIFFERENT way to solve the problem? Let's fill up the whole board.

RESPONSE: He could let his sister play with it. *(Enumeration—write under the like response, not as a separate solution.)*

Sharing with his sister and letting her play with it are kind of the SAME BECAUSE they are both letting her have a chance to play with it.

Can you think of something DIFFERENT from sharing?

RESPONSE: He could cry. *(Unclear response—clarify.)*

Tell me more about that.

RESPONSE: So his mom will feel sorry for him. *(Add to the list.)*

If the child means the boy would cry because he feels sad about not getting the sailboat, it is an irrelevant response because it does not solve the problem. In this case, however, the response is a way to get the mom to give in and therefore a relevant solution.

OK, way number one, he could ask her.

Way number two, he could say he'll share it with his sister.

Way number three, he could cry so his mom will feel sorry for him.

Who can think of way number four?

RESPONSE: I'll be good. *(Unclear response—clarify.)*

What do you mean by "be good"?

RESPONSE: I promise not to break it. *(Add to the list.)*

OK, that's DIFFERENT. Now we have four *(show four fingers)* ways this boy can try to get his mom to buy him the sailboat.

Continue to generate other alternatives as time and interest permit. When finished, summarize the different ways, holding up the appropriate number of fingers for each one. On the board, the responses given in this lesson would look like the example given.

1. He could ask her.

2. He could say he'll share it with his sister.
   He could let his sister play with it.

3. He could cry so his mom will feel sorry for him.

4. He could promise not to break it.

HINT

As mentioned earlier, it is quite common for a child who has been responding only minimally to parrot others' ideas. Such a youngster should still not be pushed for different ideas. It is more important to praise the child for having said something with a comment such as "Good, you told us, too." You can also let the child hold a puppet, then ask the puppet for an idea or tell the child to whisper the idea to the puppet.

ILLUSTRATION 18 Lesson 35

Introduction to Role-Playing

PURPOSE

To show children how to role-play an action, preliminary to later role-playing of problem situations

MATERIALS

None

TEACHER SCRIPT

Today's ICPS game is about pretending.

We are going to do things that you can see with your eyes but can NOT hear with your ears.

Make motion of brushing teeth.

What do you think I am doing? *(Let children respond.)*

Very good. I am pretending to brush my teeth.

Let's see ALL of you pretend to brush your teeth, too.

Very good.

Make motion of tying your shoe.

Now what am I doing?

Very good. I am pretending to tie my shoe.

OK, now I need a leader. *(Choose a child to come up front.)*

I am going to whisper an idea in the leader's ear, and the leader is going to pretend to do it.

Watch the leader very carefully. You guess what (he/she) is doing.

Whisper one of the following actions in the leader's ear:

- Washing face
- Blowing nose
- Reading a book
- Jumping rope
- Sweeping the floor

Repeat with new leaders as time and interest permit. Add any other actions you wish to the list, or let the leader think of a "guessable" idea. If necessary, remind the leader not to talk.

Solve a Problem

PURPOSE

To give children further practice in identifying a problem and looking for DIFFERENT ways to solve it

MATERIALS

Any storybook

TEACHER SCRIPT

Remember the last time, when we played pretend?

We pretended to do something that we could see with our eyes, but that we could NOT hear with our ears.

We're going to pretend again. Let's pretend I am going to read you a story.

Hold up any storybook.

(Child 1), stand so that you are in the way—so the other children can NOT see the storybook. *(Demonstrate position if needed.)*

OK, what's the problem here?

Yes, that's right.

(Child 1) is standing in the way of the book so not ALL of you can see.

What can (Child 2) do or say so (Child 1) will sit down and you can ALL see the storybook?

OK, that's way number one. Remember, the idea of this game is to think of lots of DIFFERENT ways.

Continue eliciting solutions as time and interest permit.

HINT

A common enumeration for this problem involves hurting. You might say, for example, "Push him down, hit him, and punch him are kind of the SAME BECAUSE they are ALL ways of hurting. Can you think of something DIFFERENT from hurting?"

Solve Another Problem

PURPOSE

To provide more practice in identifying a problem and looking for DIFFERENT ways to solve it

MATERIALS

Illustration 19

Chalkboard or easel

TEACHER SCRIPT

Show children Illustration 19.

What's going on here? What's the problem in this picture?

Allow children to suggest a number of possible problems. Write them on the chalkboard, then choose one—for example, the boys in the picture won't let the girl play.

Who can think of a way that this girl *(point)* can get the boys to let her play?

Elicit a number of possible solutions to the stated problem.

HINT

After the children have heard you classify enumerations several times, guide them in classifying for themselves. For example:

Hitting and kicking are kind of the SAME BECAUSE they can both _____. (*If needed:* Hurt OR help?)

Giving candy and giving gum are kind of the SAME BECAUSE they are both _____. (*If needed:* Giving OR taking?)

ILLUSTRATION 19 Lesson 38

Finding Solutions

MINI-DIALOGUES

The teacher in these examples uses an information-seeking, nonthreatening tone of voice and does not spend an indeterminate amount of time trying to find out who wronged whom. Children are encouraged to use feeling concepts, determine the cause of the problem, and find an alternative solution.

Situation 1: Gary and Evan are upset and crying. Each one says, "He hit me first."

Teacher: We have a problem to solve here. Gary and Evan, let's talk about this. What happened?

Gary: He hit me.

Evan: He hit me first.

Teacher: *(To Gary)* How did you feel when Evan hit you?

Gary: Mad! He messed up my paper. *(Points to the easel.)*

Teacher: *(To Evan)* How did you feel when Gary hit you?

Gary: Mad!

Teacher: Now you're both mad. Gary, do you know WHY Evan messed up your paper?

Gary: He just did!

Teacher: How can you find out WHY he messed up your paper?

Gary: *(To Evan)* WHY did you do that?

Evan: 'Cause it's my turn.

Teacher: *(To both)* OK, what can you two do now to solve the problem so you both won't be mad?

Gary: *(To Evan)* You paint here *(points to left side)*, and I'll paint here *(points to right side)*.

Situation 2: Chris knocks down Adrian's sand castle.

Teacher: What's the matter? What happened?

Adrian: He knocked my sand castle down.

Chris: He won't give me the shovel.

Teacher: We have a problem here. How do you feel, Adrian?

Adrian: Mad.

Teacher: How do you feel, Chris?

Chris: Mad.

Teacher: Is there something you can do or say so you both won't feel mad?

Adrian: No!

Chris: No!

Teacher: *(Recognizing intense emotions, decides not to dialogue with the children now.)* Let's see if anyone else can help. *(Calls Maria over and speaks to her.)* Can you help us out? Adrian wouldn't give Chris the shovel, and Chris knocked down his sand castle. What can they do or say to solve this problem?

Maria: I'm sorry.

Teacher: Who can say that?

Maria: Chris.

Teacher: Chris, is that OK?

Chris: No!

Teacher: Oh, Maria, can you give us a DIFFERENT idea?

Maria: Build a new one together.

Teacher: Chris and Adrian, what do you think of that?

Adrian: Yeah.

Chris: Let's get the other bucket.

Adrian and Chris zealously built another castle. Shortly after they started, they invited Maria to join them. This is a very different mood than if the teacher had suggested what the children should do.

There's More Than One Way

LANGUAGE ARTS: STORY COMPREHENSION

Do you remember what _____ did to _____? *(Name a specific character and repeat the character's goal.)*

What else could that person have done to _____?

Anything else?

If a story describes an interpersonal problem situation, ask the following questions:

What was the problem the people in the story had?

How did they feel?

What did they do to solve the problem?

What else could they have done?

SEQUENCING

Draw four circles, as shown.

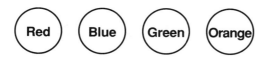

Here are some circles.

I can put them like this.

Who can think of another DIFFERENT way to put them?

Good, there's more than one way. And a still DIFFERENT way?

If desired, repeat with shapes, collage materials, or numbers. Arrange by size, shape, and so forth.

SCIENCE

There's more than one way to use water: You can drink it OR _____.
What else can you do with water?

Repeat with snow, a chair, a piece of paper, and so on.

There's more than one way to use paints: You can put your brush in
the (for example, red) jar and paint OR _____. You can put (red)
paint on top of a DIFFERENT color and make a new color.

*Demonstrate mixing colors, then let children try. (This might be easier with
fingerpaints.)*

Using ICPS Talk

Your child is starting to think about how to solve problems
on his or her own. Help your child avoid frustration and failure by
trying out this idea the next time an argument over a toy comes up
with siblings or friends.

Parent:	*(To Child 1)* What happened? What's the matter?
Child 1:	*(Responds.)*
Parent:	*(To Child 2)* What do *you* think happened?
Child 2:	*(Responds.)*
Parent:	Do you two see this the SAME way OR a DIFFERENT way?
Child 1 or 2:	*(Responds.)*

Either response, "SAME" or "DIFFERENT," can be followed with:

Parent:	Oh, we have a problem. Can you think of a way to solve it?

Adding Talk About Feelings

Helping your child identify the feelings in a problem situation
will help him or her reach a good solution. Try focusing on feelings
before you ask for a solution the next time an argument over a toy comes
up with siblings or friends.

Parent: *(To Child 1)* What happened? What's the matter?

Child 1: *(Responds.)*

Parent: *(To Child 2)* What do *you* think happened?

Child 2: *(Responds.)*

Parent: Do you two see this the SAME way OR a DIFFERENT way?

Child 1 or 2: *(Responds.)*

Either response, "SAME" or "DIFFERENT," can be followed with:

Parent: *(To Child 1)* How do you feel about this?

Child 1: *(Responds.)*

Parent: *(To Child 2)* And how do you feel?

Child 2: *(Responds.)*

Parent: We have a problem here. Can you think of a way to solve it?

CONSEQUENCES

The lessons in this section help children understand the possible consequences of a particular solution. A *consequence* is a reaction by Person B in direct relationship to an act performed by Person A. For example, if Sally hits Megan, Megan might, in consequence, choose to hit her back, tell the teacher, or not play with her anymore.

Lessons 39 through 43 help children learn to understand the sequence of events. Lessons 44 and 45 help children think about whether an idea is or is not a good one, for early evaluation of solutions to interpersonal problems. Understanding of these ideas is prerequisite to actual consequential thinking, taught in Lessons 46 through 50. The goal of consequential thinking is to help children think about what might happen next if a particular solution were carried out.

To this point, the exchanges between children and teacher have been "mini-dialogues," including some but not all of the steps in full ICPS dialoguing. After Lesson 46, in which true consequential thinking is first taught, you may begin to conduct full ICPS dialoguing in the classroom. Basically, this involves asking children "What MIGHT happen next" in addition to using the steps already described. Examples of full ICPS dialogues appear after Lesson 50.

PROCEDURE

As shown in the lessons, you can elicit consequences by undertaking the following steps:

1. State the problem or have the child state the problem.

2. Elicit alternative solutions in the usual way.

3. When a solution conducive to asking for consequences comes up, use that one. (Usually, "hit," "grab," or "tell someone" are good ones to start with.)

4. Write this solution on the left side of chalkboard or easel.

5. Say, "OK, let's make up a DIFFERENT kind of story. Pretend the child *(repeat the solution)*. What MIGHT happen next in the story?" Be sure to elicit direct consequences only, not *chain reactions*. For instance, if Sally hits Megan, Sally may continue a chain of events: Megan might hit Sally back (a direct consequence), then Sally might throw a block at her. Sally's throwing the block is a chain reaction to hitting back, not the direct consequence of Sally's first hitting Megan. If chaining occurs, point it out. For instance, you

could say, "That MIGHT happen if Megan hits Sally back. What MIGHT happen next when Sally hits Megan?"

6. Say, "Let's think of lots of things that MIGHT happen next if *(repeat solution)*. I'm going to write all the things that MIGHT happen next on the board. Let's fill up the whole board." Write these consequences in a column on the right side of the board and draw arrows from the solution to them, as the example shows.

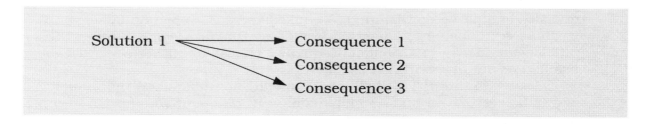

7. If necessary, probe for further consequences by asking, "What MIGHT _____ say? What MIGHT _____ do?"

8. Evaluate both positive solutions as well as negative ones. Occasionally ask, "What could _____ do so (a particular negative consequence) will NOT happen?"

ENUMERATIONS

As they do when asked for alternative solutions, children often give consequences that are variations on a theme. Classify these responses in the same way you would solutions, pointing out that the ideas are all "kind of the SAME." Ask for "something that MIGHT happen that is DIFFERENT" from the enumerated response.

UNCLEAR OR
APPARENTLY IRRELEVANT RESPONSES

Handle unclear or seemingly irrelevant responses in the same way as for alternative solutions. Find out what the child has in mind. When eliciting consequences, it is especially important to question the child as to who is doing the action. For example, Lesson 46 presents a situation where a boy wants a girl to let him feed some fish. The response "grab the food" could be either solution or consequence. If the boy grabs the food, it could be a solution to his problem. If the girl grabs the food, it could be a consequence to whatever solution is proposed. If the child means that the boy grabs the food (a solution), you can elicit a consequence by asking, "What MIGHT the girl do or say if the boy does that?"

Mystery Sequence, Part I

PURPOSE

To help children think sequentially, a precursor to anticipating what MIGHT happen next

MATERIALS

Illustrations 20 and 21

TEACHER SCRIPT

Today's ICPS game is called Mystery Sequence.

Show children Illustrations 20 and 21.

_____, come and point to the picture of what happens first.

(*If needed:* Would the girl brush her teeth first OR would she get out of bed first?)

Now point to what happens next.

You just told a story. First you get out of bed, and then you brush your teeth.

You can NOT brush your teeth and then get out of bed.

You can NOT get dressed and then get out of bed.

What else can you NOT do and then get out of bed?

Make up other possibilities, be silly, and have fun.

ILLUSTRATION 20 Lesson 39

ILLUSTRATION 21 Lesson 39

A Story

PURPOSE

To encourage story comprehension and help children understand sequencing, for later consequential thinking

MATERIALS

Any storybook

TEACHER SCRIPT

Read any storybook to the class, then reread and, at appropriate points, ask the following questions:

Recalling Events

Someone in the story (did/said) _____. *(Repeat an event or statement.)* Who (did/said) that?

What did the person (do/say) next?

And then?

Understanding Feelings

WHY do you think the person did that?

Would you have (done/said) the SAME thing OR something DIFFERENT? *(If different: What would you have done OR said?)*

How do you think the person felt when _____? *(Repeat event or statement.)*

How do you think _____ felt when _____? *(Name a different character in the story and repeat event or statement.)*

Did _____ AND _____ feel the SAME way OR a DIFFERENT way?

How do you feel about _____? *(Repeat event or statement.)*

Does anyone feel a DIFFERENT way about _____? *(Repeat event or statement.)*

Mystery Sequence, Part II

PURPOSE

To help children learn to think sequentially with regard to an interpersonal problem

MATERIALS

Illustrations 22 and 23

TEACHER SCRIPT

Today's ICPS game is called Mystery Sequence, just like the game we played before.

Show children Illustrations 22 and 23. Two sequences are possible:

Sequence 1

1. One boy grabs the truck, and the other boy cries. (Illustration 23)
2. The crying boy gets up, and the two start fighting over the truck. (Illustration 22)

Sequence 2

1. The boys are fighting over the truck. (Illustration 22)
2. One boy wins out, leaving other boy crying. (Illustration 23)

_____, come point to the picture showing us what happened first.

Now point to the picture that shows us what happened next—you know, second.

Put the picture the child points to first to the left of the other picture.

What is happening in the picture you pointed to first? Can you tell us?

Then what happened? What is happening in the picture you pointed to second?

Good, you told us a story.

Does anyone see a DIFFERENT story?

Elicit as many different stories as you can. Children may offer a different sequence or express variations on the same sequence. Encourage children to think of as many endings as they are able by asking them what else could have happened next.

ILLUSTRATION 22   Lesson 41

ILLUSTRATION 23   Lesson 41

More ICPS Words: If-Then

PURPOSE

To teach the terms IF-THEN as a precursor to consequential thinking

MATERIALS

None

TEACHER SCRIPT

Today's ICPS game is about something new. We're going to talk about the words IF-THEN.

IF I say your name, THEN you may jump.
(Child 1): May (Child 1) jump?
Yes, (Child 1) may jump. Go ahead and jump.

IF I say your name, THEN you may hop.
(Child 2): May (Child 2) hop?
Yes, (Child 2) may hop. Go ahead and hop.

IF I say your name, THEN you may stretch. *(Demonstrate.)*
(Child 3): May (Child 3) stretch?
Yes, (Child 3) may stretch. Go ahead and stretch.

Now listen carefully. I'm going to change the game a little.

IF I put my hand in water, THEN it will get wet. *(Demonstrate, if possible.)*

IF (Child 4) closes (his/her) eyes, THEN (he/she) can NOT see. Go ahead and close your eyes. Can you see?

IF you close your mouth, THEN you can NOT eat.

IF you eat too much candy, THEN what MIGHT happen?

IF you do NOT brush your teeth, THEN what MIGHT happen?

IF you run inside, THEN what MIGHT happen?

IF you touch a hot stove, THEN what MIGHT happen?

Let children name a few of their own IF-THENS.

Mystery Sequence, Part III

PURPOSE

To give children additional practice in sequential thinking

MATERIALS

Illustrations 24–26

TEACHER SCRIPT

Today we have a new Mystery Sequence game.

Show children Illustrations 24, 25, and 26. Two sequences are possible:

Sequence 1

1. Girl watches dog. (Illustration 24)

2. Girl kicks dog. (Illustration 25)

3. Dog bites girl. (Illustration 26)

Sequence 2

1. Girl watches dog. (Illustration 24)

2. Dog bites girl. (Illustration 26)

3. Girl kicks dog. (Illustration 25)

_____, come point to the picture showing us what happened first.

If the picture the child chooses is not already in the left-hand position, ask the child to move it there.

What happens next?

Put that picture here. *(Point to the middle position.)*

And then what happens?

Put that picture here. *(Point to the right-hand position.)*

Tell us the story you just made with the pictures. *(Let child respond.)*

Good, you told us a story. Does anyone see a DIFFERENT story?

Elicit as many different stories as you can. Children may offer a different sequence or express variations on the same sequence.

After the (girl kicked the dog/dog bit the girl), what else could have happened next?

Encourage children to think of as many endings as they can.

ILLUSTRATION 24   Lesson 43

ILLUSTRATION 25 Lesson 43

ILLUSTRATION 26   Lesson 43

Remembering Sequences

Draw three circles on chalkboard or easel. Color with chalk or crayons. Erase chalkboard or flip easel paper.

Who can put up the SAME pattern as the one I just made? (Pattern 1)

Who can put up a DIFFERENT pattern? (Pattern 2)

How is Pattern 2 *(point)* DIFFERENT from Pattern 1 *(point)*?

Add more circles, or repeat with animal shapes, fat and skinny people, or other objects.

A Good Idea?

PURPOSE

To encourage early consequential thinking

MATERIALS

Illustration 27

TEACHER SCRIPT

For today's ICPS game, we're going to talk about what IS and what is NOT a good idea.

Show children Illustration 27.

Look at these pictures carefully.

(Child 1), come and point to a picture of someone who is doing something that is NOT a good idea.

Regardless of the illustration the child points to, ask the following questions:

Tell us what the child is doing.

WHY is that NOT a good idea?

IF the child does that, THEN what MIGHT happen next?

IF that happens, THEN how MIGHT the child feel? *(Be sure to ask how both children might feel if the swing picture is chosen.)*

Who else thinks that this is NOT a good idea?

WHY do you think that?

Is that BECAUSE the SAME or DIFFERENT from the BECAUSE (Child 1) said?

What could the child in the picture do that IS a good idea?

WHY is that a good idea? BECAUSE _____.

What MIGHT happen next if the child does that?

Then how do you think the child will feel?

Does anyone feel that this IS a good idea?

Does anyone else feel a DIFFERENT way about this? (*If appropriate:* DIFFERENT children feel a DIFFERENT way about the SAME thing. Is that OK?)

Ask another child to identify a different picture of a child doing something that is not a good idea. Repeat the previous line of questioning for the new picture.

Now we're going to change the game a little.

(Child 2), come and point to a picture of someone who is doing something that IS a good idea.

Regardless of the illustration the child points to, ask the following questions:

WHY is that a good idea?

If you feel the SAME way about this, raise your hand.

If you feel a DIFFERENT way about this, raise your hand.

If you feel a DIFFERENT way, WHY do you think that is NOT a good idea?

Ask another child to identify a different picture of a child doing something that is a good idea. Repeat the previous line of questioning for the new picture.

ILLUSTRATION 27 Lesson 44

Is That a Good Idea, Place, or Time?

SOME HELPFUL QUESTIONS

When a child is running indoors:

Is running indoors a good idea?

What MIGHT happen next?

IF that happens, THEN how will you feel?

What can you do that IS a good idea?

When a child is drawing on the table:

Is that a good place to draw?

WHY is that NOT a good place?

Where IS a good place to draw?

When a child is putting toys away in the wrong place:

Is that a good place for the big blocks?

Where IS a good place?

When a child is in the way of others at storytime:

Is that a good place to stand?

WHY is that NOT a good place?

Where can you stand that IS a good place? (Or: What can you do so others can see the storybook?)

When a child won't dress properly for cold weather:

Is going out in the snow without your boots a good idea?

Why NOT? BECAUSE _____.

What else do you need to put on when you go out in the snow?

When a child interrupts:

Is this a good time to talk to me?

Why NOT?

Can I talk to you AND to _____ at the SAME time?

What can you do while you wait?

MINI-DIALOGUES

After children become familiar with the concepts illustrated in these examples, you can shorten most of your communication to "Is that a good idea? A good place? A good time?" The children will know what you mean.

Situation 1: Lawrence brings his ball to storytime.

Teacher: Is this a good place to bring a ball?

Lawrence: I guess not.

Teacher: WHY do you think this is NOT a good place?

Lawrence: It's storytime.

Teacher: That's true. What MIGHT happen if you bring that here?

Lawrence: It will bother everybody.

Teacher: Can you think of a DIFFERENT place to put the ball so it won't bother everybody?

Lawrence thinks for a moment, then takes the ball to the corner of the room. No resistance, no power play, no problem emerges.

Situation 2: Alice is painting at the easel without an apron.

Teacher: Alice, is it a good idea to paint at the easel without an apron?

Alice: *(Does not answer.)*

Teacher: What MIGHT happen if you paint without an apron?

Alice: My dress will get dirty.

Teacher: What can you do so your dress will NOT get dirty?

Alice: Put on my apron.

By age 4, children know what might happen. They do not need to be told—again.

Situation 3: Nancy is riding her tricycle too fast.

Teacher: Is riding so fast a good idea?

Nancy: Yep!

Teacher: I think you're teasing me. What MIGHT happen if you ride too fast?

Nancy: I MIGHT fall off.

Teacher: Can you think of a DIFFERENT way to ride that bike?

Nancy: Yep! *(Rides off more slowly.)*

Situation 4: A group of children are standing at a table, listening to a conversation between a visitor and a child. The children are holding their pencils with the points precariously close to one another.

Teacher: Are your pencils in a good place when you're standing so close to one another?

Children: *(Laugh.)*

Teacher: Can anyone think of a DIFFERENT place for your pencils?

Child: *(Placing pencil behind ear)* Now I won't poke anybody.

The other children follow suit, and no more needs to be said.

Situation 5: Lamont leaves a small truck in the middle of the book area.

Teacher: Is that a good place to leave the truck?

Lamont: No.

Teacher: Why NOT?

Lamont: You don't want it there.

Teacher: What MIGHT happen if you leave it there?

Lamont: I'll be in trouble.

Teacher: WHY is it NOT a good idea to leave it there?

Lamont: I don't know.

Teacher: If someone walks into the book corner, and does NOT see the truck, what MIGHT happen?

Lamont: He could fall on it.

Teacher: Where IS a good place to put the truck?

Lamont: In the block corner.

Note how the teacher emphasizes the internal reason that someone might fall, not the external idea of being in trouble. The teacher could have extended the discussion of consequences by asking, "What MIGHT happen if he falls?"; "How MIGHT he feel if he hurts himself?"; and "Where can you put this truck so he doesn't fall and doesn't feel SAD?"

Situation 6: Shawn is standing too close to some other children who are playing catch.

Teacher: Shawn, is that a good place to stand?

Shawn: No, I MIGHT get hit.

No more needs to be said.

Situation 7: Some children are jumping rope in front of the school door.

Teacher: Children, is this a good place to jump rope?

Child 1: Yeah!

Teacher: Can people get in and out of the school if you're right in front of the door?

Child 1: No.

Teacher: Can you think of a DIFFERENT place to jump rope?

Child 2: Let's go over by the fence.

In this example, the teacher recognizes that the children's motive is to jump rope, not to keep people from going in and out of the school. If the children had been in imminent danger of being harmed, the teacher would have moved them quickly, then talked about the problem in ICPS style.

Advanced Concepts

LANGUAGE ARTS: STORY COMPREHENSION

Familiar Stories

Who remembers what happens next? (*If appropriate:* Was it a good idea for the person to do that? WHY or why NOT?)

Unfamiliar Stories

What do you think happens next? Who can guess?

OK, let's see what's next.

MATH

IF you had only one leg, THEN you could NOT _____.

What can someone do who has one leg?

What else?

IF you had only one arm, THEN you could NOT _____.

What can someone do who has one arm?

What else?

SCIENCE

IF the wind is blowing very hard, THEN what MIGHT happen to a leaf lying on the ground?

IF it is warm outside, THEN the snow will melt and turn to water.

IF I bring snow inside, THEN what will happen to the snow? The SAME thing OR something DIFFERENT?

IF a bird breaks his wing, THEN he can NOT _____.

IF it never rained, what would happen to the flowers?
What else would happen IF it never rained?

HEALTH/HYGIENE

What MIGHT happen if . . .

You do NOT brush your teeth?

You eat the SAME food ALL of the time?

You do NOT sleep at night?

In the winter, you go out in the snow, but do NOT put on boots and mittens?

SAFETY

Is it a good idea to ride in a car on the sidewalk?

WHY do you think that?

Where IS a good place for the car to be?

Is it a good idea to cross the street when the light is red?

WHY?

You can cross the street on a _____ light. (*If needed:* Green OR purple?)

Is it a good idea to stick your arm out of the bus window?

WHY?

Where IS a good place to keep your arm?

Is it a good idea NOT to stay with the group on a class trip?
WHY?

Let children think of their own examples.

Is That a Good Idea?

Your child has been learning to think about whether an idea IS or is NOT a good one. Try asking the following questions.

If your child is running inside:

Is running inside a good idea?

What MIGHT happen next?

How will you feel IF that happens?

How will I feel?

What can you do that IS a good idea?

If your child is climbing on furniture:

Is that a good idea?

What MIGHT happen next?

How will you feel IF that happens?

How will I feel?

What can you do that IS a good idea?

If your child is drawing on walls (or playing with water in the living room, or fingerpainting without newspaper):

Is drawing on walls a good idea?

What MIGHT happen next?

How will you feel IF that happens?

How will I feel?

Where can you draw that IS a good idea?

Try to focus on internal versus external consequences when asking what might happen next. If the child says, "I'll get punished," ask, "What else?" Try to encourage answers like "I'll get hurt," "The couch will get dirty," and so on.

What Can I Do While I Wait?

PURPOSE

To help children cope with frustration when their needs cannot be met immediately

MATERIALS

Illustration 28

TEACHER SCRIPT

Show children Illustration 28.

Who can tell me what the mother in this picture is doing? (*If needed:* She is putting pictures in her photo album.)

What is this girl *(point)* trying to do? (*If needed:* She is asking her mom to read her a story.)

Is it a good idea for the girl to ask her mom to read when she is busy doing something else?

No, it is NOT a good idea. What IS a good idea? (*If needed:* Is it a good idea to wait until her mom gets finished with what she is doing?)

Yes, it IS a good idea to wait until her mom gets finished with what she is doing.

WHY is it a good idea to wait? BECAUSE _____.

Does anyone have a DIFFERENT BECAUSE?

What MIGHT happen IF the girl does NOT wait? (*If needed:* How will her mom feel?)

Now listen carefully. Here is a new question: What can this girl do while she waits?

(After the first response) OK, that's *one* thing she can do. Who can think of something DIFFERENT she can do?

Encourage children to give a number of alternatives.

Who can tell us a time when you had to wait for something?

What could you do while you wait for that?

Invite a number of children to offer suggestions.

HINT

Point out, in language your group can understand, that finding something else to do while you wait can make waiting much easier.

ILLUSTRATION 28   Lesson 45

Helping Children Wait

MINI-DIALOGUES

Situation 1

Zachary: I want the clay.

Teacher: I can't get it now BECAUSE I'm helping Tyrone.

Zachary: But I want it now!

Teacher: I know you do. When I'm finished with Tyrone I'll get it for you. Can you think of something DIFFERENT you can do now while you wait?

Zachary: *(Thinks for a moment.)* I'll go paint.

Zachary zealously grabs an apron and paints at the easel. This is a markedly different result than if the teacher had said, "Why don't you go paint?"

Situation 2

Sarah: *(Interrupts teacher.)* Mr. Brown, can I have some clay?

Teacher: I can't get it for you now. I'm talking to Ms. Claybourne. Can you think of something DIFFERENT to do while you wait?

Sarah: No!

Teacher: I bet if you think hard, you can think of something to do.

Sarah: I'll cook dinner (in the doll corner).

Whose idea was this?

Helping Your Child Wait

How can you use ICPS words when:

- Your child interrupts you when you're talking on the phone?
- Your child wants you to read a story at an inconvenient time?
- Two children are vying for your attention at the same time?

Try asking the following questions:

Can I talk to you AND to my friend at the SAME time?

Can you think of something DIFFERENT to do until I can talk to you?

Can I read to you AND cook dinner at the SAME time?

Can you think of something DIFFERENT to do until I can read to you?

Can I hear both of you at the SAME time?

What can you two do so I can listen to both of you?

YOUR IDEAS

_____

_____

_____

_____

What Might Happen Next? Part I

PURPOSE

To illustrate that what we do and say affects what others do and say

MATERIALS

Illustration 29

Chalkboard or easel

TEACHER SCRIPT

NOTE

After this lesson, you may integrate full ICPS dialoguing in the classroom. See examples after Lesson 50.

Show children Illustration 29.

Today's ICPS lesson is about these children.

Let's pretend the problem here is that this boy *(point)* wants this girl *(point)* to let him feed the fish.

What can the boy do or say so the girl will let him feed the fish?

I'm going to put ALL your ideas on this side *(the left side)* of the chalkboard.

Elicit three or four solutions. Write each one as given, as the example shows.

1. He could push her.
2. He could give her candy.
3. He could ask her.

Now listen very carefully. We're going to change the question. IF the boy pushes the girl out of the way, THEN what MIGHT happen next?

I'm going to write what you think MIGHT happen next over here. *(Point to the right side of the board.)*

RESPONSE: She'll hit him. *(Write this consequence on the right side of the board. Very dramatically, draw an arrow as shown.)*

1. He could push her. ⟶ 1. She'll hit him.

OK, she MIGHT hit him. What else MIGHT happen next?

Elicit additional consequences, adding them to the list as given and drawing arrows from the solution as shown.

1. He could push her. 1. She'll hit him.
2. She'll cry.
3. She'll tell her mother.
   She'll tell her father.

Remember to watch for and classify enumerations (for example, telling her father). Place them with the like consequence, as the previous example shows. Classify by saying, "Telling her mother and telling her father are kind of the SAME BECAUSE they are both telling someone. What MIGHT happen next that is DIFFERENT from telling someone?"

(When a number of consequences have been generated) Look at ALL the things that can happen just from this one act, pushing the girl out of the way.

Maybe SOME of us think pushing her out of the way IS a good idea.

If you think pushing her out of the way IS a good idea, raise your hand.

_____, WHY do you think that IS a good idea? *(If needed: BECAUSE _____.)*

OK, maybe it IS a good idea BECAUSE _____. *(Repeat child's reason.)*

Ask each child who raises his or her hand to state a reason.

Maybe SOME of us think pushing her out of the way is NOT a good idea.

If you think pushing the girl out of the way is NOT a good idea, raise your hand.

_____, WHY do you think that's NOT a good idea? (*If needed:* BECAUSE _____.)

OK, maybe that's NOT a good idea BECAUSE _____. *(Repeat child's reason.)*

Ask each child who raises his or her hand to state a reason.

HINT

If a child gives a *solution* (for example, "The boy could grab the food") say, "That's what the *boy* could do to solve this problem" and write that solution on the left side. Repeat: "We want to know what the *girl* might do or say if the boy pushes her out of the way." If you are unsure whether a response is a solution or a consequence, ask, "Who would do that?" If the child says the boy would do that, the response is a solution; if the girl, it is a consequence.

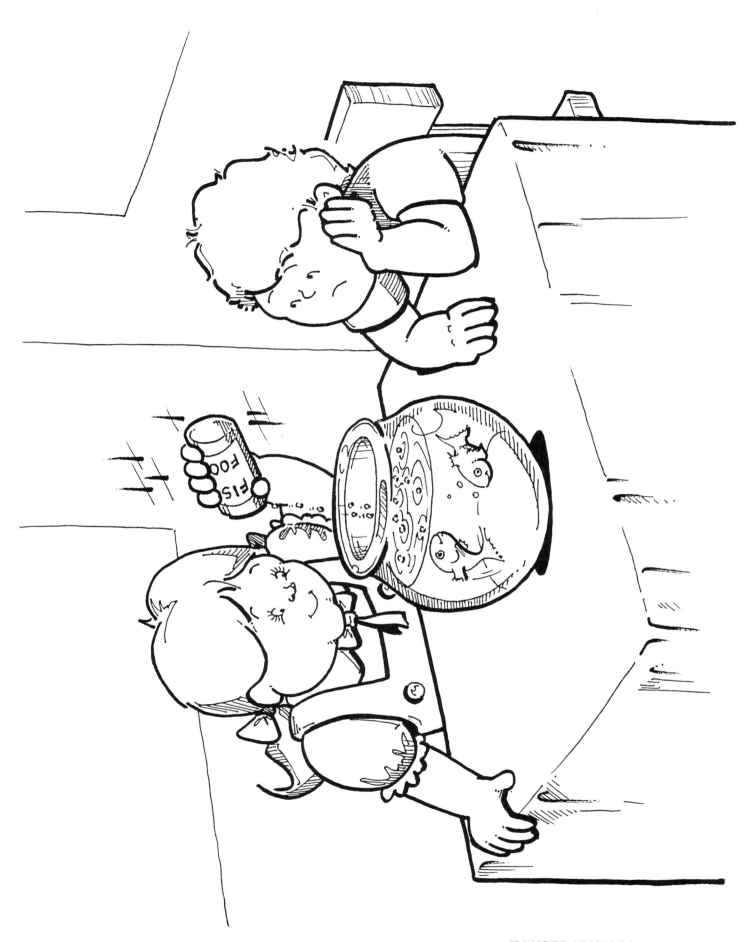

ILLUSTRATION 29   Lesson 46

What Might Happen Next? Part II

PURPOSE

To strengthen the idea that what we do and say affects others

MATERIALS

Illustration 30

Chalkboard or easel

TEACHER SCRIPT

Show children Illustration 30.

Let's pretend the problem is that this girl on top of the slide *(point)* wants to come down, and the girl at the bottom *(point)* won't get off.

What can this girl *(point)* do or say so this girl *(point)* will get off?

I'm going to put ALL your solutions on this side *(the left side)* of the chalkboard.

Elicit three or four solutions. Write each one as given, as the following example shows.

1. She could push her off.
2. She could say, "Get off!"
3. She could tell her mother.
4. She could ask her.

Now listen carefully. Let's talk about the idea to push the girl off the slide.

IF the girl at the top pushes her off, THEN what MIGHT happen next?

RESPONSE: She'll hit (punch, kick) her. *(Write this consequence on the right side of the board. Very dramatically, draw an arrow from the solution to it.)*

OK, she MIGHT hit her. That's *one* thing that MIGHT happen.

What else MIGHT happen? I'm going to write what else MIGHT happen on the right side.

Elicit as many consequences as possible, adding them to the list as given and drawing arrows as shown in the example.

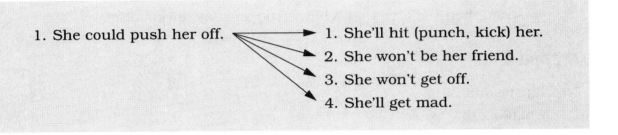

1. She could push her off.
1. She'll hit (punch, kick) her.
2. She won't be her friend.
3. She won't get off.
4. She'll get mad.

(When a number of consequences have been generated) Look at ALL the things that MIGHT happen just from this one act, pushing the girl off the slide.

Who thinks pushing her off IS a good idea?

WHY?

Who thinks pushing her off is NOT a good idea?

WHY?

OK. Now let's talk about solution number two, to say, "Get off!"

Repeat this process with the other solutions, including positive ones. The next example shows two possible consequences of a positive solution.

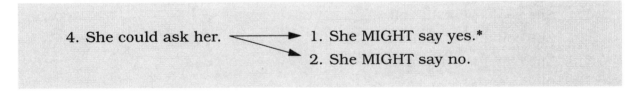

4. She could ask her.
1. She MIGHT say yes.*
2. She MIGHT say no.

*Kids have fun chanting, "She MIGHT say yes/she MIGHT say no" in response to the solution "She could ask."

ILLUSTRATION 30 Lesson 47

A Story

PURPOSE

To review a number of ICPS concepts

MATERIALS

Any storybook

TEACHER SCRIPT

Read any storybook to the class. Then reread and, at appropriate points, ask the following questions:

Who remembers what _____ (did/said) when _____?
(Name a character and describe an event from the story.)

Do you think that IS or is NOT a good idea?

WHY do you think that?

Ask these first three questions about several characters in the story.

How MIGHT _____ feel when _____?
(Name a character and describe an event.)

What MIGHT happen next?

Elicit both positive and negative outcomes. If a negative outcome, ask:

What else can the person do so that will NOT happen?

What Might Happen Next? Part III

PURPOSE

To guide children in thinking about interpersonal consequences

MATERIALS

Any two hand puppets (for example, Allie the Alligator and Whipple the Whale)

A crayon and a piece of paper

TEACHER SCRIPT

Today we're going to make up a story together, and Allie and Whipple will help you.

Place the crayon in Whipple's mouth and the piece of paper in front of you.

Uh-oh, Whipple is scribbling all over Allie's paper. (*Scribble with crayon in Whipple's mouth. Pull Allie's mouth down.*)

How does Allie feel?

How can we find out? (*If needed:* Let's ask her.)

Let a child ask Allie how she feels.

Teacher:	Allie, WHY do you feel (ANGRY/SAD)?
Allie:	BECAUSE _____. Does anyone know WHY I feel (ANGRY/SAD)?
Teacher:	We know that Allie feels (ANGRY/SAD). Let's make up what MIGHT happen next in this story. (*If needed:* What MIGHT Allie do or say next?) Remember, Whipple scribbled on her paper.
Children:	(*Respond.*)
Teacher:	That's *one* thing that MIGHT happen. Who can think of something DIFFERENT that MIGHT happen? That's the idea of this game—to think of lots of DIFFERENT things that MIGHT happen.

Elicit as many consequences as you can, asking such questions as "What else MIGHT Allie do?" and "What else MIGHT Allie say?"

Teacher: Oh, Whipple, Allie is still angry. You'll have to think of something DIFFERENT—a DIFFERENT way to solve this problem.

Whipple: Allie, do you like to paint?

Allie: Yes.

Whipple: Let's paint together.

Allie: OK.

Teacher: Allie and Whipple painted together at the easel and laughed and laughed. *(Imitate laughter.)*

Whipple: I didn't mean to scribble on your paper. I really like you.

Teacher: *(To the group)* How do Allie and Whipple feel now? Yes, HAPPY.

Let children pair off and make up a problem that the puppets might have. Ask for only one solution so several pairs can have a turn acting their situation out for the group.

What Might Happen Next? Part IV

PURPOSE

To give children further practice in thinking about interpersonal consequences

MATERIALS

Illustration 31

Chalkboard or easel

TEACHER SCRIPT

Show children Illustration 31.

Does anyone see something in this picture that might be a problem? (*If needed:* Let's say this boy—*point*—wants the teacher to look at his painting, too.)

Elicit and write down solutions as given until one is conducive to naming consequences. Draw arrows, classify enumerations, and clarify in the usual way. The following example shows some possible responses.

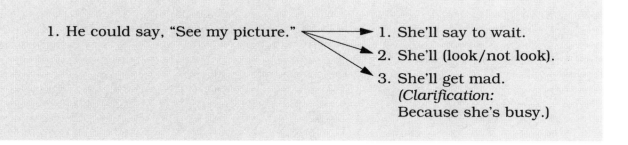

1. He could say, "See my picture."
   1. She'll say to wait.
   2. She'll (look/not look).
   3. She'll get mad.
      (Clarification:
      Because she's busy.)

Discuss whether each consequence given is or is not a good idea, as in Lessons 46 and 47.

ILLUSTRATION 31 Lesson 50

ICPS Dialoguing

The following three dialogues illustrate how to apply full ICPS dialoguing.

I HAD IT FIRST

Non-ICPS Dialogue

(Teacher solves the problem)

Teacher: *(To Child 1)* Why are you pulling that book away from (Child 2) like that? You know you'll tear it.[1]

Child 1: I had it first!

Child 2: I had it first!

Teacher: Now who had it first?[2]

Child 1: Me!

Child 2: No, me!

Teacher: If you can't share it, I'll have to take it away. If you don't learn to share, you won't have any friends. Children should learn to share. We share things at this school.[3]

ICPS Dialogue

(Child solves the problem)

Teacher: *(To Child 1)* What's the matter? What's the problem?[1]

Child 1: *(Pulling the book from Child 2)* She won't let me see the book.

Child 2: I had it first!

Child 1: No, I had it first!

Teacher: What MIGHT happen if you pull the book like that?[2]

Child 1: It MIGHT break.

Teacher: What can you two think of to do when two children want the SAME book at the SAME time?[3]

Child 1: It's mine!

Teacher: *(To Child 2)* Can you think of a way to solve this problem?[4]

Child 2: I look at it, then her.

Child 1: Let's look at it together.

Child 2: OK.[5]

NOTES

[1] Not really concerned about "why"; tells children what they should think.

[2] She will never know.

[3] They probably didn't hear a word of this.

[1] Elicits child's view of the problem.

[2] Elicits consequences; doesn't get stuck on "who had it first."

[3] Elicits solutions.

[4] Turns to the other child for help.

[5] Happy with their own solution, the children are much more likely to carry it out.

IT'S MINE

Teacher:	Cheryl, what's happening here? That will help me understand the problem better.	*Elicits the child's view of the problem.*
Cheryl:	The clay is mine.	
Teacher:	What happened when you grabbed the clay?	*Guides the child to consider the consequences of her actions.*
Cheryl:	Vicki hit me.	
Teacher:	How did Vicki feel when you grabbed?	*Elicits other's feelings.*
Cheryl:	Mad.	
Teacher:	How did *you* feel when Vicki hit you?	*A very dynamic question: "Someone cares how I feel."*
Cheryl:	Mad.	
Teacher:	Grabbing is *one* thing you can do. Can you think of something DIFFERENT you can do so she won't hit you and you both won't be mad?	*Guides the child to think of a solution in light of consequences.*
Cheryl:	*(To Vicki)* Can I have the clay?	
Vicki:	No!	
Teacher:	Oh, you'll have to try again. Can you think of a DIFFERENT idea?	*Encourages the child not to give up too soon—there is more than one way.*
Cheryl:	*(To Vicki)* If you let me have the clay, I'll build you a castle. Do you like that?	*The child is using the Do You Like Game (see Lesson 29).*

Happy with their own solution, the children felt proud, and the teacher didn't have to explain why they should share.

HE HIT ME

Teacher:	Shawn, what happened?	*Elicits the child's view of the problem.*
Shawn:	Tom hit me.	
Teacher:	Do you know WHY Tom did that?	*Stimulates causal thinking.*
Shawn:	No.	
Teacher:	How can you find out?	*Encourages Shawn to talk to Tom about the problem.*
Shawn:	I could ask him.	
Teacher:	Go ahead and ask him.	*Encourages putting thought into action.*
Shawn:	*(To Tom)* WHY did you hit me?	
Tom:	You called me a dummy.	
Teacher:	Shawn, are you feeling HAPPY now or are you ANGRY?	*Helps the child to think about his own feelings.*
Shawn:	ANGRY!	
Teacher:	Tom, how do you feel?	*Guides the other child to think of his feelings.*
Tom:	ANGRY.	
Teacher:	You two have a problem. Shawn called Tom a dummy and Tom hit Shawn. Can either of you solve this problem?	*Guides children to think of solutions in light of consequences.*
Shawn:	I could say I won't call you a dummy anymore.	
Teacher:	Go ahead and try that.	*Shawn does, and the two go off and play together.*

This teacher may have known why Tom hit Shawn, but it was more important for the children to think the problem through for themselves. This approach avoids resistance and potential teacher-child power plays.

Adding Consequences

Try adding talk about consequences before asking for a solution the next time an argument over a toy comes up with siblings or friends.

Parent:	*(To Child 1)* What happened? What's the matter?
Child 1:	*(Responds.)*
Parent:	*(To Child 2)* What do you think happened?
Child 2:	*(Responds.)*
Parent:	Do you two see this the SAME way OR a DIFFERENT way?
Child 1 or 2:	*(Responds.)*

Either answer, "SAME" or "DIFFERENT," can be followed with:

Parent:	*(To Child 1)* How do you feel about this?
Child 1:	*(Responds.)*
Parent:	*(To Child 2)* And how do you feel?
Child 2:	*(Responds.)*
Parent:	*(To Child 1)* When you grabbed the toy, what happened next?
Child 1:	*(Responds.)*
Parent:	Can either of you solve this problem so you both will NOT feel mad and you won't fight?

I Had It First

Here's an example of a parent's handling a problem situation without using ICPS talk.

Mom:	Why are you two fighting?
Sarah:	I had it first.
Debbie:	I had it first.
Mom:	Now look, I can't help you if you don't tell me who really had it first.

She'll never know. . .

Sarah:	Me, me!
Debbie:	I was playing with it, and she took it.
Mom:	If you two grab like that you won't have any friends and you'll break toys, and you won't have anything to play with. Mommy will be mad and you'll both end up in your rooms.

The children probably didn't hear a word of this. Later. . .

Mom:	You're grabbing again. Don't you learn? You know Mommy is mad. What do I have to do to teach you to share and be nice to each other? If you don't learn to be nice to each other, how are you going to learn to be nice to other people?

They probably didn't hear this either.

To see a different way of handling the situation, see the next page.

Here's the same problem situation, but this time the parent uses ICPS talk.

Mom: What's happening? What's the matter?

Sarah: It's mine. I had it first.

Debbie: No, I had it first.

Mom: Sarah, how do you feel when Debbie grabs things from you?

Sarah: Mad.

Mom: Debbie, how do *you* feel when Sarah grabs from you?

Debbie: Mad.

Mom: Now you're both mad. Grabbing is one way to get your doll back. What happens next when you grab?

Debbie: We fight.

Mom: Can either of you think of a DIFFERENT way so you both won't be mad and you won't have to fight?

Sarah: We can shake hands.

Debbie: We can play together.

Sarah: Let's put the blue dress on her.

A 4-year-old and a 6-year-old thought about their feelings and decided how to solve this problem. Had their mother suggested they shake hands and play together, would they have?

I Forgot...

Here's an example of a parent's handling a problem situation without using ICPS talk.

Dad: Richard, what's this trash doing under your bed?

Richard: I forgot to throw it out.

Dad: Well, do it this minute! And don't ever let me see this here again!

The next night...

Dad: Richard, I can't believe this! What did I say about the trash? *(Pauses.)* I'm talking to you! What's this doing here?

Richard: I don't like trash. I'm...

Dad: Richard, your job is throwing out the trash. We all have our chores in this family. Don't you want to be part of this family?

Richard: *(Sulking)* OK.

Demands. Explanations. Nothing about the child's feelings or a thought that Richard might have his own problem here. The more the father nags, the worse the whole conflict becomes.

To see a different way of handling the situation, see the next page.

Here's the same problem situation, but this time the parent uses ICPS talk.

Dad: This trash bag is still under your bed. How come?

Richard: 'Cause I don't like taking it out.

Dad: How come?

Richard: 'Cause I'm afraid.

Dad: Of what?

Richard: The dark.

Dad: You never told me that.

Richard: I was afraid you'd call me a baby.

Dad: Richard, you don't have to throw out the trash. But you're part of this family, and I want you to do something to help take care of the house. Can you think of some way you can help?

Richard: *(Pauses.)* I can feed the dog.

Dad: Is that what you'd like to do?

Richard: Yeah.

Where's the solution? The trash isn't out. But that's not really the problem. The problem is getting the child to take responsibility. Once the father saw that, he let Richard make a choice—take charge. Richard and his father are both going to be proud of Richard's taking care of the dog.

It's Mine

Here's an example of a parent's handling a problem situation
without using ICPS talk.

Mom: Becky, why did you do that?

Becky: What?

Mom: Grab that toy from Ruth.

Becky: 'Cause it's mine.

Mom: Give it back!

Becky: I don't want to. It's mine.

Mom: Why not play with your dolls?

Becky: I want my sailboat.

Mom: Play together. Or take turns. Grabbing isn't nice.

Becky: I want my boat now!

Mom: If you don't share, Ruth will get mad and she won't be your
        friend.

Becky: But, Mom . . . she won't give it to me.

Mom: You can't just grab things. Would you like it if she did that
        to you?

Becky: *(Pauses.)* No.

Mom: Tell her you're sorry.

*If parents don't think their children listen, do kids think no one listens to them?
If parents really listen to their children, would they learn something new?*

To see a different way of handling the situation, see the next page.

Here's the same problem situation, but this time the parent uses ICPS talk.

Mom: What's happening? What's the matter?

Becky: She's got my boat. She won't give it back.

Mom: Why do you need it now?

Becky: She's had a long turn.

Becky had already shared her toy, and that's how she saw the situation.

Mom: How do you think Ruth feels when you grab from her?

Becky: Mad, but I don't care. It's mine.

Mom: What did Ruth do when you grabbed it?

Becky: Hit me.

Mom: How did that make you feel?

Becky: Mad.

Mom: So you're mad, and Ruth's mad, and she hit you. Can you think of a DIFFERENT way to get your boat back, so you both won't be mad...and so Ruth won't hit you?

This gets Becky thinking about what she and her friend could do.

Becky: I could ask her.

Mom: And then?

Becky: She'll say no.

Mom: MAYBE. What else could you do so she'll give back your boat?

Becky: *(Pauses.)* I could let her have my animals.

Becky's mother didn't try to make 4-year-old Becky share her toy. She shifted the whole objective to accommodate Becky's view of the problem—getting her toy back. She freed Becky to think for herself.

He Hit Me

Here's one example of a parent's handling a problem situation without using ICPS talk.

Todd: Mommy, Bobby hit me.

Mom: Oh, I'm sorry.

Todd: Two times.

Mom: When?

Todd: In school.

Mom: I'll talk to the teacher. Don't worry.

Mom solves this problem. Now Todd doesn't have to think about it anymore.

In this next example, the parent still isn't using ICPS talk.

Sam: Peter hit me.

Dad: Hit him back.

Sam: He'll punch me harder.

Dad: Then punch him harder. Don't be timid.

Sam: But I'm afraid.

Dad: If you don't learn to defend yourself, kids will keep hitting you.

Sam: OK.

Who's doing the thinking here?

In the next example the advice is different, but the approach is the same.

Ralph: Paul hit me.

Mom: What did you do then?

Ralph: Hit him back.

Mom: Don't hit back. You might hurt someone. Just tell the teacher.

Ralph: He'd call me a tattletale.

Mom: If you don't tell her, he'll keep hitting you.

Ralph: OK.

Although they have good intentions, the parents in the previous three examples are concerned with the problem only from their point of view. How did their children see it? Why were they hit, anyway?

To see a different way of handling the situation, see the following dialogue.

Here's the same problem situation, but this time the parent uses ICPS talk.

Steven: Dad, Tommy hit me.

Dad: Do you know WHY?

Steven: No.

Dad: It will help me understand better if you can think about that.

Steven: I called him stupid.

Dad: How come? What's bothering you?

Steven: *(Pauses.)* Dad, he tore up my book.

Dad: Oh, I see, he tore your book, you called him stupid, and he hit you.

Steven: Yeah.

Dad: Calling him stupid is *one* thing you can do. Can you think of something DIFFERENT to do so he won't hit you?

Steven: I could tear *his* book.

Dad: And what MIGHT happen then?

Steven: We'll fight.

Dad: Is that what you want to happen?

Steven: No.

Dad: Can you think of a DIFFERENT way?

Steven: I could say, "I won't be your friend."

This dad didn't tell or suggest what to do. He let his 4-year-old son come to his own conclusion—a sensible one.

SOLUTION-CONSEQUENCE PAIRS

The lessons in this section help teach children how to generate solution-consequence pairs. By doing so, children will ultimately be able to choose from among a number of solutions on the basis of their most likely consequences.

PROCEDURE

As shown in the lessons, the steps for teaching solution-consequence pairs are as follows:

1. State the problem or have the child state the problem.
2. Elicit one solution to the problem.
3. Ask for a consequence of that solution.
4. If the consequence is relevant, elicit a second solution.
5. Ask for the consequence of the second solution, and so on, as the example shows.

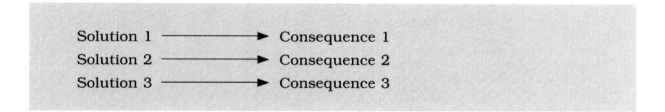

Solution 1 ⟶ Consequence 1
Solution 2 ⟶ Consequence 2
Solution 3 ⟶ Consequence 3

ENUMERATIONS AND UNCLEAR OR APPARENTLY IRRELEVANT RESPONSES

Treat enumerations and apparently irrelevant responses as you would for alternative solutions or consequences. Distinguish chain reactions from consequences if necessary.

What Might Happen If I Do That? Part I

PURPOSE

To introduce the idea of solution-consequence pairs and encourage immediate evaluation of problem solutions

MATERIALS

Illustration 32

Chalkboard or easel

TEACHER SCRIPT

Show children Illustration 32.

Today's ICPS problem is about this boy *(point).*

He wants the fire fighter to give him a ride on the fire truck.

What does this boy want the fire fighter to do?

Right, give him a ride. OK, who can tell me *one* way this boy could do that?

RESPONSE: He might ask. *(Solution—write this and other solutions as given on the left side of the chalkboard.)*

Now listen carefully. Here's the question.

IF this boy asks the fire fighter, THEN what MIGHT happen next? *(If needed:* What MIGHT the fire fighter do or say?*)*

RESPONSE: The fire fighter might say no. *(Consequence—write this and other consequences as given on the right side of the board. Draw an arrow from solution to consequence, as the example shows.)*

1. The boy might ask. ⟶ 1. The fire fighter might say no.

267

OK. Now let's think of a DIFFERENT way for the boy to get the fire fighter to let him have a ride.

He could ask him OR _____?

RESPONSE: Say, "Just for a little while." *(Solution—add to the list on the left side.)*

THEN what do you think the fire fighter MIGHT do?

RESPONSE: He might say OK. *(Consequence—add to the list on the right side.)*

He MIGHT say OK. Now let's think of way number three.
The boy could ask him OR say, "Just for a little while" OR _____?

RESPONSE: Take money out of his mom's pocketbook. *(Unclear response—clarify.)*

How will that help solve this problem?

RESPONSE: Then give it to the man. *(Solution—add to the list.)*

Note that this is an example of what first appears to be an irrelevant solution which, when probed, actually reflects relevant thinking by the child.

What about way number four?

RESPONSE: He might cry. *(Unclear response—clarify.)*

Tell me more about that.

RESPONSE: Because the man won't let him have a ride. *(Not a solution.)*

OK, he MIGHT cry. What can he do or say so the man will give him a ride?

Note that this is an example of "cry" being not a solution to obtain sympathy, but a response to frustration.

He could ask the fire fighter, and THEN the fire fighter MIGHT say no.

He could say, "Just for a little while," and THEN the fire fighter MIGHT say OK.

He could take money out of his mom's pocketbook and give it to the fire fighter, and THEN the fire fighter MIGHT spend the money and still say no.

That's three ways the boy could try. Who can think of way number four?

Continue with this line of questioning as long as time and interest permit. On the board, the responses given in this lesson would look like the example provided.

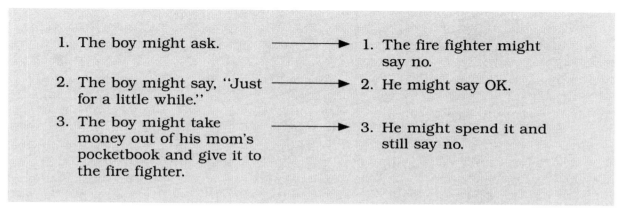

1. The boy might ask. ⟶ 1. The fire fighter might say no.

2. The boy might say, "Just ⟶ 2. He might say OK.
for a little while."

3. The boy might take ⟶ 3. He might spend it and
money out of his mom's still say no.
pocketbook and give it to
the fire fighter.

HINT

Note that the teacher repeats the children's solutions and consequences but *never* adds any new ideas.

ILLUSTRATION 32   Lesson 51

What Might Happen If I Do That? Part II

PURPOSE

To further encourage immediate evaluation of problem solutions

MATERIALS

Illustration 33

Chalkboard or easel

TEACHER SCRIPT

Show children Illustration 33.

Who can make up a problem—you know, something that is wrong in this picture? (*If needed:* Let's say this girl on the bike wants this boy in the wagon to get out of her way.)

Who can think of way number one to solve this problem?

I'm going to write your idea here on the left side of the chalkboard.

RESPONSE: She could ask him. *(Solution—write this on the left side of the board.)*

You just told us she could ask him to get out of the way.

Now listen carefully to this question. IF the girl does that, THEN what MIGHT happen next?

I'm going to put what MIGHT happen next here on the right side.

RESPONSE: He'll get out of the way. *(Consequence—write this on the right side of the board.)*

OK, here's the game.

You tell me something the girl could do or say so the boy will get out of her way—then tell me what MIGHT happen next if she does that. (*If needed:* What MIGHT the boy do or say IF the girl does that?)

Who has way number two?

RESPONSE: She could give him candy. *(Solution—add to the list.)*

OK, she could give him candy.

What MIGHT happen next?

RESPONSE: He'll eat it. *(Unclear response—clarify.)*

Yes, he MIGHT eat it.

How would that help the girl get the boy to move? (*If needed:* Do you think the boy would get out of the way?)

Note that the response "He'll eat it" is irrelevant because it is not related to the desired consequence of having the boy get out of the way. Therefore, it is not added to the list.

OK, who has way number three?

RESPONSE: She could punch him. *(Solution—add to the list.)*

And what do you think MIGHT happen next IF the girl punches the boy?

RESPONSE: He'll punch her back. *(Consequence—add to the list.)*

Continue eliciting solutions and their immediate consequences as time and interest permit. On the board, the responses given in this lesson would look like the example provided.

1. She could ask him. ⟶	1. He'll get out of the way.
2. She could give him candy. ⟶	2. He'll get out of the way.
3. She could punch him. ⟶	3. He'll punch her back.

HINT

When asking for a solution, point dramatically to the girl. When asking for a consequence, point dramatically to the boy.

ILLUSTRATION 33   Lesson 52

What Else Can I Do?

PURPOSE

To help children experience whether their solutions to an actual problem are successful

MATERIALS

Enough classroom objects, puppets, or trinkets so that each child has one

TEACHER SCRIPT

Give each child a classroom object, puppet, or trinket, each different from the other. Encourage the children to find ways to end up with the one they want.

(*If grabbing or hitting occurs*) How does that make _____ feel? (*If needed:* HAPPY, SAD, or ANGRY?)

What MIGHT _____ do or say if you grab that from him?

What MIGHT happen next?

What else can you do or say so _____ will give you the object (he/she) has?

If not successful: Can you think of a DIFFERENT idea?

If successful: How does that make you feel?

After each child ends up with the desired object, pick an object that one child is holding (for example, a stuffed bear) and ask, "Who is NOT holding a bear?" If the child holding the bear raises a hand, say to the child, "Now listen carefully: Who is NOT holding a bear?" Repeat with each object. Then ask each child to name an object that he or she does NOT have. Finally, alternate between have and do NOT have.

Additional Advanced Concepts

LANGUAGE ARTS: STORY COMPREHENSION

While reading a story, apply full ICPS dialoguing. At appropriate points, ask the following questions:

What's the problem that _____ has? *(Name a specific character.)*

How did the person feel when _____? *(Describe an event.)*

How did another person feel when _____? *(Describe an event.)*

What did this person do to try to solve the problem?

What happened next?

What else could (he/she) have tried?

And then what?

What's a still DIFFERENT idea (he/she) could try?

MUSIC TIME

Apply the technique used in Lesson 53 by giving out musical instruments randomly.

(To Child 1) What instrument do you have?

(To Child 2) What instrument do you have?

(To the group) Do (Child 1) and (Child 2) have the SAME instruments?

No, they are _____.

Ask a few other pairs of children the same questions.

(To the group) Look around and see if anyone has an instrument that you would like to have for music time—one that you do NOT have.

Does anyone see one?

(To any child) Who has an instrument you would like to have?

Can you think of a way to get _____ to let you have that instrument?

If refused: Oh, you'll have to think of something DIFFERENT.

If still refused: Do you see a DIFFERENT instrument you would like?

Let several children try this. In game form, children asked to exchange their instruments usually do so.

Puppet Story

PURPOSE

To illustrate that different people like different things and to review ICPS concepts

MATERIALS

Any two hand puppets (for example, brother and sister puppets)

TEACHER SCRIPT

Brother: *(Cries.)*

Sister: I wonder WHY my brother is so SAD. *(Looks at brother.)* WHY are you feeling so SAD?

Brother: How do you know I'm SAD? How can you tell?

Sister: I can see with my eyes that you are crying.

Brother: I'm going to put my hands over your eyes. *(Puts hand over sister's eyes.)* Now you can't see me crying.

Sister: I can still tell you're SAD.

Brother: *(Crying)* How?

Sister: I can hear you with my ears. *(To the group)* I wonder WHY he's so SAD. How can I find out?

Children: Ask him.

Sister: Yes, I'll ask him. *(To the group)* Let's ask him together: "WHY are you so SAD?"

Children: WHY are you so SAD?

Brother: WHY do you think I'm so SAD?

Sister: BECAUSE you can NOT go out and play?

Brother: No, that's NOT why I'm so SAD.

Sister: MAYBE it's BECAUSE your friend did NOT come today?

Brother: No, that's NOT why I'm so SAD.

Sister: *(To the group)* Does anybody know WHY he is so SAD?

- MAYBE _____. *(Repeat first response.)*
- MAYBE _____. *(Repeat second response.)*
- MAYBE _____. *(Repeat third response.)*

Continue as long as children give responses.

Sister: I wonder how I can make him feel better. *(Pauses, then, excitedly)* I know! Going to the zoo would make you HAPPY, right?

Brother: No!

Sister: No? Going to the zoo would make *me* HAPPY. I thought that would make *you* HAPPY, too.

Brother: I do like the zoo. But I went to the zoo already today. I do NOT want to go to the zoo again now.

Sister: Oh, I didn't know you just went to the zoo. Would going for a walk make you HAPPY?

Brother: No, I do NOT like to walk.

Sister: Walking makes *me* HAPPY. I thought walking would make *you* HAPPY, too.

Brother: DIFFERENT people like DIFFERENT things. You like to walk. I do NOT like to walk.

Sister: *(To the group)* Do you have any ideas? *(To one child)* What makes _____ HAPPY?

Child: Candy.

Sister: *(To child)* Candy makes *you* HAPPY. *(To brother)* Does candy make you HAPPY, brother?

If brother disagrees: Candy does NOT make my brother HAPPY.

If brother agrees: You and my brother like the SAME thing.

Sister: Who has a DIFFERENT idea to make my brother HAPPY?

Ask each child who offers a suggestion, "Does that make you HAPPY?" then ask the brother puppet the same question. If a child dominates the discussion, point out that it is FAIR to take turns and that each child can have one turn. Have the brother puppet sometimes agree and sometimes disagree with the children's suggestions. When children run out of suggestions, summarize the ideas that make the brother puppet happy:

Sister: *(To brother)* Does _____ make you HAPPY?

Brother: Yes, _____ makes me very HAPPY. AND _____, AND _____, AND _____. More than one thing makes me HAPPY. You asked me, and you found out what makes me HAPPY. Also, by asking, you found out what does NOT make me HAPPY. Now that you have made me HAPPY, I would like to make you HAPPY. Would you like to play with me?

HINT

Let the brother puppet agree with the suggestions of a more inhibited child so as not to discourage that child's responses.

Dialoguing With Puppets

PURPOSE

To introduce role-play dialoguing for real problems

MATERIALS

Any two hand puppets (for example, Allie the Alligator and Whipple the Whale)

TEACHER SCRIPT

Teacher: *(To Allie)* What happened? What's the matter?

Allie: Whipple called me a dummy.

Whipple: I did not.

Allie: You did too!

Teacher: OK, you both know if Whipple did or did NOT call you a dummy. Do you two see the problem the SAME way OR a DIFFERENT way?

Allie: A DIFFERENT way.

Teacher: Allie, how do you feel now?

Allie: ANGRY.

Teacher: Whipple, how do you feel now?

Whipple: ANGRY.

Teacher: Which of you can think of a way to solve this problem? Something you can do so you both will NOT feel ANGRY.

Let children take the parts of the puppets and finish the story.

HINT

Puppets can help engage children in ICPS dialoguing when actual problems arise in the classroom or when children report problems from home.

A Story

PURPOSE

To encourage solutions and consequential thinking and to stress that DIFFERENT people can feel DIFFERENT ways about the SAME things

MATERIALS

Any storybook

TEACHER SCRIPT

Read any storybook to the class, then reread and, at appropriate points, ask the following questions:

Do _____ and _____ have a problem to solve? *(Name two characters from the story.)*

Do they see the problem the SAME way OR a DIFFERENT way?

What can one person do or say that MIGHT solve this problem?

Is that a good idea?

What MIGHT happen next if (he/she) does that?

Sample Story

Read Ernie's Big Mess, *by Sarah Roberts (Random House/Children's Television Workshop, n.d.), then at the following specified points, ask these questions:*

After: ''Bert and Ernie are best friends. They live together. Bert is neat. Ernie is messy.''

What does it mean to be messy?

Do Bert and Ernie feel the SAME way OR a DIFFERENT way about being messy?

When Ernie is messy, how does Bert feel?

After: ''Ernie stops smiling. 'Bert does not want me here anymore. I guess I will go away.' ''

How does Ernie feel now?

After: "Ernie climbs into the nest. 'Ouch!' says Ernie. 'This is not a nice place to sleep. It is full of sticks.' "

Do Ernie and Big Bird feel the SAME way OR a DIFFERENT way about sleeping in a nest?

Do you feel the SAME way about sleeping in a nest as Ernie does OR as Big Bird does?

Do you feel the SAME way as Big Bird about sleeping in a nest?

Why do you feel that way about sleeping in a nest? BECAUSE _____.

After: " 'A big soft bed?' yells Oscar. 'Soft beds are yucchy!' Bang! goes the lid of the trash can."

Do Ernie and Oscar feel the SAME way OR a DIFFERENT way about sleeping in a soft bed?

Do you feel the SAME way as Ernie OR as Oscar about sleeping in a soft bed?

What is the problem that Bert and Ernie are having?

How did they solve this problem? You know, so Bert was NOT ANGRY anymore.

What else could Ernie do or say to solve this problem?

Is that a good idea?

What MIGHT happen next if he does that?

Anything else?

Elicit solution and consequence pairing.

288

What's Your Problem? Part I

PURPOSE

To help children evaluate and choose one solution over another on the basis of their understanding of consequences

MATERIALS

Chalkboard or easel

TEACHER SCRIPT

Today's ICPS game is about a problem you have.

You know, something goes wrong between you and a friend, or you and your brother or sister, or you and your mom or dad—anyone, really.

Who can tell us a problem you had with someone? (*If needed:* MAYBE you got into a fight, someone snatched something, someone wouldn't give you a turn with something you wanted, or you got into trouble for something.)

Let children generate a number of problems, then select one. For example, "My brother won't stop breaking my toys."

OK, now listen very carefully.

Let's think of DIFFERENT ways to help (Child 1) solve this problem.

Let's start with (Child 1). Tell us a way you could get your brother to stop breaking your toys.

If relevant: OK, that's *one* way. (*Write this solution on the left side of the chalkboard.*)

Now we're going to think of a new way, a DIFFERENT way to solve that problem.

Who's got way number two? (*Show two fingers.*)

If relevant: Now we have two ways (*Write this solution on the left as well.*)

Now listen again. We're going to think about what MIGHT happen next IF (Child 1) really did those things.

(Repeat Solution 1.) IF (Child 1) really did that, THEN what MIGHT happen next?

If relevant: OK, that MIGHT happen. *(Write this consequence on the right side of the board.)*

What else might happen? *(Write the second consequence on the right as well.)*

At this point, the board will look like the following example.

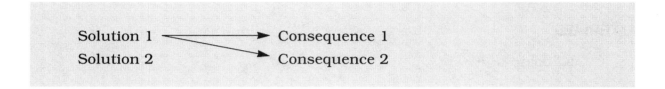

OK, now let's talk about your second idea.

(Point to and repeat Solution 2.) IF (Child 1) really did that, THEN what?

And what else?

Now the board will look like the next example.

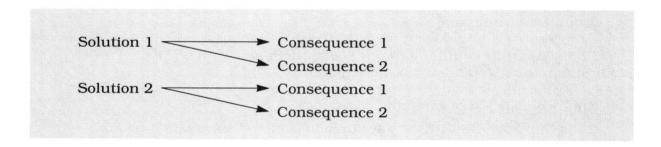

OK, listen very carefully. (Child 1) could *(repeat Solution 1)* OR (he/she) could *(repeat Solution 2).*

(Child 1), if you could choose one of these ideas, and only one, which one would you choose?

WHY?

Would anyone choose to _____? *(Repeat the other solution.)*

Did (Child 2) and (Child 1) choose the SAME idea OR a DIFFERENT idea?

Elicit a third solution and its consequences if time and interest permit. Tell the group that others will have a chance to tell about a problem on a different day.

What's Your Problem? Part II

PURPOSE

To give children additional practice in choosing one solution over another on the basis of their understanding of consequences

MATERIALS

Chalkboard or easel

TEACHER SCRIPT

Remember when we talked about a problem (Child 1) had?

Who has a DIFFERENT problem you would like to tell us about?

OK, (Child 2) just told us _____. *(Repeat problem.)*

Today we're going to think of a way to solve that problem and THEN what MIGHT happen next.

Who's got way number one?

If relevant: That's *one* way. *(Write this solution on the left side of the chalkboard.)*

Now listen carefully.

IF (Child 2) really (did/said) that, THEN what MIGHT happen next?

If relevant: OK, that MIGHT happen. *(Write this consequence on the right side of the board.)*

Now listen again, very carefully.

What else can (Child 2) do or say to solve this problem?

Something I can put over here. *(Point to the left side of the board.)*

If relevant: OK, now we have two ways. *(Add this solution to the list.)*

Now listen again. IF (Child 2) really (did/said) that, THEN what? *(Point to the spot to the right of Solution 2.)*

If relevant: OK, that MIGHT happen. *(Add this consequence to the list.)*

On the board, the solutions and their paired consequences would look like the example given.

Solution 1 ————————▶ Consequence 1

Solution 2 ————————▶ Consequence 2

Continue solution and consequence pairing as time and interest permit. When no more solution-consequence pairs are offered:

(To Child 2) Which idea do you like best?

WHY?

(To the group) Who likes the SAME idea as (Child 2)?

Who likes a DIFFERENT idea?

WHY?

What's Your Problem? Part III

PURPOSE

To give children practice in role-playing actual problems

MATERIALS

Any two hand puppets (for example, Allie the Alligator and Whipple the Whale)

TEACHER SCRIPT

Here I have Allie and Whipple. They are going to help us solve a problem today.

Who would like to pretend a problem that Allie and Whipple are having?

Choose two children, one for each puppet.

Now (Child 1) and (Child 2), go in the corner and make up your problem. Then come and let Allie and Whipple tell us what it is.

(When children are ready) OK, Allie, tell us what the problem is. OK, Whipple, choose someone to tell you *one* way you two can solve this problem.

Let Allie and Whipple call on children to give solutions. Pick one or two solutions, then ask for consequences and choices of "best" solution.

HINT

Children can learn to use the puppets to role-play actual problem situations. Use this technique when real problems come up in the classroom.

APPENDIX A

Guidelines for Continued ICPS Teaching

Teaching does not stop once the formal ICPS lessons have been completed. If children are to associate how they think with what they do, you must continue to make frequent use of the ICPS dialoguing approach when interacting with children informally in the classroom. This association may be critical to how problem-solving thinking can guide behavior. It is also important to apply ICPS principles consistently whenever opportunities arise.

The following general suggestions can help you keep ICPS alive in your classroom after the lessons are over:

1. Continue using puppets to help dialogue actual problems (see Lesson 55).

2. Use puppets to let children role-play actual or hypothetical problems (see Lesson 59). As puppets try to solve the problem, let them call on other children to help.

3. Apply ICPS teaching to the stories you read or reread in class. At any point, ask children if they remember what happens next, or, for a new story, to guess what might happen next. Let children choose puppets and act out any part of a story they like.

4. Repeat any lesson the children enjoyed or need more of. Whenever possible, let a child lead the activity.

Quiz yourself periodically on how ICPS is working for you as a teacher. Ask yourself whether you can think of a time when:

1. You recognized a problem with the children in your class

    a. by seeing but not hearing or asking
    b. by hearing but not seeing or asking
    c. by asking, but not seeing or hearing
    d. by two or all three of these ways

2. You made a child in your class feel

    a. happy
    b. sad
    c. angry

3. A child in your class made you feel

   a. happy
   b. sad
   c. angry

4. You learned something you didn't know about a child through ICPS dialoguing.

5. When a child or children were having a problem, you thought you knew what the problem was, but because you used dialoguing you found out it was actually something quite different.

You can also use the ICPS Teacher Self-Evaluation Checklist, which immediately follows, to help you evaluate your ability to apply ICPS principles in various interpersonal situations. Duplicate the checklist and monitor your use of the ICPS approach either daily or weekly. Over time, average your score within each category as you use the checklist. As your score decreases for Categories A through C, and increases for Category D, you are increasing your use of the ICPS approach.

ICPS TEACHER SELF-EVALUATION CHECKLIST

Date(s) _____

Rating Scale: 1   2   3   4   5
                 Never   Sometimes   Always

(Today/this week) I found that with most children, I:

A. Demanded, commanded, belittled, punished   Score _____

Examples   Sit down!
             You can't do that!
             You know you shouldn't _____!
             How many times have I told you _____!
             Give it back!

B. Offered suggestions without explanation   Score _____

Examples   You can't go around hitting kids.
             Why don't you ask him for it?
             Children must learn to share.

C. Offered suggestions with explanation, including talk of feelings   Score _____

Examples   If you hit, you MIGHT lose a friend (get hurt).
             If you grab, she won't let you play with her toys.
             You shouldn't do that. It's not nice (FAIR).
             You'll make him ANGRY if you do that.

D. Guided children to think of feelings, solutions, consequences   Score _____

Examples   What's the problem? What happened?
             How do you think I (a child) feel(s) when _____?
             What happened (MIGHT happen IF) _____?
             What could you do so that would NOT happen?
             Do you think that IS or is NOT a good idea?
             (*If not a good idea:* Can you think of
             a DIFFERENT way to _____?)

ICPS Dialoguing Reminders

Post the following pages in your classroom to help remind yourself and other teachers to use ICPS dialoguing when real problems arise during the day. As the dialogues in the lessons suggest, it is important to be flexible. The steps presented here are meant to serve only as a guideline.

Happy ICPSing!

CHILD-CHILD PROBLEMS

STEP 1: **Define the problem.**

What happened? What's the matter?
That will help me understand the problem better.

STEP 2: **Elicit feelings.**

How do you feel?
How does _____ feel?

STEP 3: **Elicit consequences.**

What happened when you did that?

STEP 4: **Elicit feelings about consequences.**

How did you feel when _____?
(*For example:* He took your toy/she hit you)

STEP 5: **Encourage the child to think of alternative solutions.**

Can you think of a DIFFERENT way to solve this problem
so _____?
(*For example:* You both won't be mad/she won't hit you)

STEP 6: **Encourage evaluation of the solution.**

Is that a good idea or NOT a good idea?
If a good idea: Go ahead and try that.
If not a good idea: Oh, you'll have to think of something DIFFERENT.

STEP 7: **Praise the child's act of thinking.**

If the solution works: Oh, you thought of that all by yourself. You're a
good problem solver!
If the solution does not work: Oh, you'll have to think of something
DIFFERENT. I know you're a good thinker!

TEACHER-CHILD PROBLEMS

Can I talk to you AND to _____ at the SAME time?

Is that a good place to _____?

(*For example:* Draw/leave your food)

Can you think of a good place to _____?

Is this a good time to _____?

(*For example:* Talk to your neighbor/talk to me)

When IS a good time?

How do you think I feel when you _____?

(*For example:* Don't listen/throw food/interrupt me)

Can you think of something DIFFERENT to do until _____?

(*For example:* You can fingerpaint/I can get what you want/I can help you)

APPENDIX C

ICPS Word Concept Illustrations

Display the following illustrations on classroom walls or bulletin boards. They will serve as reminders to use ICPS words during the day.

Is   Not

Which girl *is* jumping?
Which girl is *not*
jumping?

Some   All

Are *some* of the people happy or are *all* of the people happy?

And   Or

Is this boy laughing **and** clapping **or** is he laughing **and** sitting?

Same

Different

Are these boys doing the **same** thing or something **different**?

Good idea

Not good idea

Is running inside a
good idea
or ***not a good idea***?

Good place

Not good place

Is this a **good place** or **not a good place** to stand?

Good time

Not good time

Is this a **good time** or **not a good time** to ask this boy to play?

APPENDIX D

Summary of ICPS Behavior Management Techniques

Experience suggests that, if teachers are sensitive to "difficult" behaviors and ready to accept and incorporate them and the child into the training process, the program moves smoothly and both teacher and children are able to enjoy it every step of the way. The following techniques, given as hints in the lessons, will help you manage these behaviors during ICPS lesson time.

SHY, NONRESPONSIVE BEHAVIORS

1. Encourage extra use of body movements, as in Lessons 2 and 6. If nonresponsiveness is extreme, guide the child by saying, "Let's shake our heads together" in answer to a yes-or-no question (for example, "Are you jumping?"). This technique helps the child move beyond complete passivity.

2. Offer one-word choices. For example, in response to a question such as "How do you feel when . . .?" offer "HAPPY or SAD?"; "SAD or ANGRY?"; and so forth. To a question such as "We are NOT doing the SAME thing as Tommy. We are doing something _____?" offer the choice, "SAME or DIFFERENT?" In this way, the child does not have to respond to an open-ended question or verbalize a whole sentence.

3. Encourage the child to draw feelings and problem situations. The child then does not have to express them verbally.

4. Let the child point in lessons where this is appropriate (for example, in Lesson 26, where illustrations are chosen). Again, the child is participating without having to speak.

5. Let the child respond through a puppet character. "Allie the Alligator" may express ideas, even though Keshia does not. After getting used to responding as the puppet, the child may begin responding, however slowly, as herself.

6. In the lessons devoted to problem-solving skills, avoid the temptation to offer solutions or consequences yourself. Many shy nonresponders will begin to offer their own ideas soon after they feel comfortable verbalizing.

7. Praise any level of response. When given the opportunity to respond and generous praise, most shy nonresponders blossom.

DISRUPTIVE OR OBSTINATE BEHAVIORS

1. After the ICPS word concepts SAME and DIFFERENT are introduced (Lessons 6 and 7), use them to bring a child who is disruptive or obstinate back into the group. You might say, for example, "Robert is fussing. The rest of us are jumping. Is Robert doing the SAME thing OR something DIFFERENT from the rest of us?" Using the concepts this way avoids a power play, which only propels the child to fight back or become more obstinate.

2. After feeling word lessons (for example, Lessons 11 and 12) have been conducted, ask the child how she is feeling. Let the group try to think of ways to help the child feel better. Using the Do You Like Game (Lesson 29) can also help. One child who was pouting was asked, "Do you like horses?" The child smiled and came right back to the lesson. If the child does not respond to such inquiries, do not push. Asking the child to join or leave the group may only cause a negative association with the lessons.

3. Be careful to distinguish disruptive or obstinate behavior from true upset. In addition, avoid taking so much time dealing with a disruptive or obstinate child that other group members become restless.

DOMINATING BEHAVIORS

1. A child who tells long, drawn-out stories can create a loss of interest in the rest of the group. Use the word DIFFERENT (Lessons 6 and 7) after it has been introduced. For example, you might say, "Dennis just had a turn. Can someone DIFFERENT have a turn?" This technique helps the dominating child become more aware of others' needs.

2. If you think the child will not be upset, use the words NOT (Lesson 3) and FAIR (Lessons 32 and 33): "If Dennis has had a very, very long turn and Rashad has NOT had a turn, is that FAIR?" This technique is another way of keeping the dominating child in the lesson.

3. Realize that extremely verbal children often unintentionally dominate the group. Handle them with care, using the techniques already presented to avoid alienating them.

SILLY BEHAVIOR

1. Respond to children who intentionally give irrelevant or opposite answers, or who laugh hysterically or make faces or funny gestures, by saying quietly, "Oh, you're just teasing me" and continuing with the lesson. Negative reactions tend to perpetuate silly behavior.

2. Shy nonresponders may parrot others' responses; if so, they should not be pushed to provide another answer. However, if a child repeats others' responses in a silly manner, or just to gain attention, she may be told directly, "I know you can think of something DIFFERENT." This kind of attention helps the child learn.

3. If a child continues to be silly, you may simply ignore him. If he is also being disruptive or obstinate, you may also use the techniques listed earlier. When the child does respond normally, be sure to praise the new behavior. Silly behavior due to lack of ability to contribute often diminishes as children learn the concepts of the program.

ABOUT THE AUTHOR

Photograph by Nora Alba

Myrna B. Shure, Ph.D., is professor of psychology at Drexel University (formerly MCP Hahnemann University) in Philadelphia. Her *I Can Problem Solve* (ICPS) series for schools is the original interpersonal problem-solving program for children, supported by 25 years of research.

The ICPS programs and Dr. Shure's pioneering research with George Spivack have received numerous awards including the Lela Rowland Prevention Award (1982) from the National Mental Health Association; the Division of Community Psychology's Distinguished Contribution Award (1984) from the American Psychological Association (APA); and two awards from special APA task forces that recognized ICPS as a national model prevention program (1986, 1993). ICPS was also selected as a Model Violence Prevention Program by the Departments of Education and Justice in the 1999 Annual Report on School Safety.

Dr. Shure is also the author of three ICPS parenting books: *Raising a Thinking Child* (Pocket Books, 1996), *Raising a Thinking Child Workbook* (Research Press, 2000), and *Raising a Thinking Preteen* (Henry Holt, 2000). She is a frequent consultant to the media on issues relating to social adjustment and interpersonal competence in our nation's youth.

The ICPS approach has been recognized as an Exemplary Mental Health Program by the National Association of School Psychologists (1998); an Evidenced-Based Prevention Intervention by the Substance Abuse and Mental Health Services Administration (1999); and an Exemplary Juvenile Delinquency Prevention Program by the Strengthening America's Families Project, University of Utah, in collaboration with the Office of Juvenile Justice and Delinquency Prevention (1997) and the Center for Substance Abuse Prevention (2000). In addition, ICPS has been recognized as a promising approach by the Center for the Study and Prevention of Violence, Blueprints for Violence Prevention (1999), and the Expert Panel on Safe, Disciplined, and Drug-Free Schools, U.S. Department of Education (2001).